English for

BUSINESS LIFE

IAN BADGER PETE MENZIES

Self-study guide

...ate

Acknowledgements

The authors would like to thank the following for their advice and support in the preparation of ***English for Business Life***: Simon Ross, Lucy Brodie, Keith Dalton, Jo Barker, Graham Hart, Teresa Miller, John Russell and Fiona Walker. Special thanks to Valerie Lambert for her work on the Business Grammar Guide.

We would also like to thank our business 'students' from organisations including UPM-Kymmene Oyj, Metso Paper, BEMIS, Vattenfall, the International Maritime Organisation, GE Finance, ABN Amro (Investment Bank), Dresdner Kleinwort Wasserstein (UK), Panasonic Europe, Nokia and Marketing Akademie Hamburg for providing the inspiration and feedback that underpins ***English for Business Life***.

First published 2006 by Marshall Cavendish Education

Marshall Cavendish is a member of the Times Publishing Group

Marshall Cavendish Education
119 Wardour Street
London W1F 0UW
www.mcelt.com/business

Designed by Hart McLeod, Cambridge

Printed and bound by Times Offset (M) Sdn. Bhd. Malaysia

Photo acknowledgements

Pg 5 C Devan/Zefa/Corbis, Pg 7 Ariel Skelty/Corbis, Pg 10 Alamy/OnRequest, Pg 12 Yellow Dog Productions/Getty, Pg 15 Stillpictures, Pg 18 Sebastien Starr/Getty, Pg 21 David Sacks/Getty, Pg 24 Arcaid, Pg 27 Norman Jung/Zefa/Corbis, Pg 30 Taxi/Getty, Pg 33 Courtesy Cameron Balloons, Pg 36 David Oliver/Getty, Pg 38 Lonelyplanetimages.com, Pg 41 JLP/Sylvia Torres/Corbis, Pg 44 Ray Kachatorian/Getty, Pg 47 Taxi/Getty, Pg 50 Rex, Pg 54 Rex. Pg 57 Ed Holub/Photex/Zefa/Corbis, Pg 60 VCL/Chris Ryan/Getty, Pg 63 Ronnie Kaufman/Corbis, Pg 66 4cornersimages.com, Pg 69 Gregory Bajor/Alamy, Pg 72 Tibor Bognor/Corbis, Pg 74 R.Holz/Zefa/Corbis, Pg 77 Falko Updarp/Zefa/Corbis, Pg 80 John Francis Bourke/Getty, Pg 83 Steven Peters/Getty, Pg 86 Superstock/Alamy, Pg 88 BananaStockAlamy

Contents

Introduction

The Self-study guide is part of the ***English for Business Life*** business English course. It follows the ***English for Business Life*** syllabus and language programme. Each level of the ***English for Business Life*** course has a Self-study guide – this is the intermediate level.

This Self-study guide can be used:

- as a standalone self-study course
- in class to supplement ***English for Business Life*** course work
- for homework
- as a key component of the 'comprehensive' study track (the ***English for Business Life*** course has three study tracks: fast, standard and comprehensive)
- as practice material for learners who are following general English courses and need practice in everyday business English.

Each unit begins with a recorded summary of useful phrases and includes:

- clear study notes
- realistic practice exercises.

At the back of the guide are:

- an easy-to-follow Business Grammar Section
- a glossary of key business-related terms
- clear answers and audioscripts to support the practice exercises.

The recorded material is available on two CDs which are included with the book. The recordings include standard native-speaker accents and examples of speakers from different parts of the world; this reflects the fact that English is used as the international language of business.

Recommended study procedure

- Listen to the Useful Phrases as often as possible and repeat where appropriate. These recordings are of speakers with standard UK/US accents.
- Work through the Study Notes and refer to the Business Grammar Section as indicated.
- Note down words and phrases that are particularly useful to you.
- Use a good dictionary to check the meanings of unfamiliar words.
- Work through the exercises and then check the answers at the back of the book.

Some study tips

- Approach language learning with the same level of commitment that you would any other project in your work. It can be useful to prepare a 'contract' with yourself in which you agree to do a certain amount of work on your English per day/week/month.
- In our view, 'little and often' is more effective than occasional long study sessions. When you travel, take your Self-study guide with you. You can work with it at times that suit you – for example, when you are in your car, at home or on a plane. Journeys can provide a great opportunity for uninterrupted practice.
- Use new language and phrases whenever possible. Live practice is the best way to learn new terms.
- Keep a paper/electronic study file in which you note down the language most relevant to your everyday needs.
- Relate the language presented and practised to your particular area of business. If there are terms you need which are not included in the material, do some research on the Internet, and consult English-speaking colleagues, friends and teachers.
- Make use of the English-speaking media – in particular facilities on the Internet. Listen to the radio and TV. Read professional journals and newspapers. Subscribe to an English magazine which interests you from a work or leisure point of view.

UNIT 1

Everyday business contacts

Some useful phrases

Listen to the recording and repeat

Hello, is that Mrs Friedman?
Speaking. Hi, it's Jan here.
Are you busy? Is this a good time to talk?
Can you talk?
Yes, go ahead.

Is it about Thursday?
I'm sorry, I'm in a meeting.
Can I call you back this afternoon?

Could I speak to the sales manager?
Is Harry Pontia there?
He's on another line.
I'm afraid he isn't available.

We open at 8am Eastern Standard Time.
That's eleven o'clock your time.
You're three hours ahead of us.
It's a public holiday today.
There's no one in the office.

Can I take a message?
Can you give Maria a message?
Could you tell her that Rosa called?
Could you ask her to call me?

Do you have any time this afternoon?
No, but I have some free time tomorrow.
So, have we covered everything?
Is there anything else?
I think that's everything. Thanks for calling.

How often do you use English in your job?
I use English every day.
I sometimes have problems on the phone.
The company's official language is English.

Study notes

Hello, is that Mrs Friedman?
Hi, it's Jan here.
Some phrases for opening a phone call.

I'm sorry, I'm in a meeting.
Some other reasons why you cannot speak on your mobile:
The reception is bad. *There's no signal.*
Sorry, I'm very busy at the moment. Can I call you back?

We open at 8am Eastern Standard Time.
That's eleven o'clock your time.
Some other phrases for referring to time differences:
It's 2 o'clock my time. *What time is it in Bishkek?*
I'll call you at 3pm your time.
There are more examples in Business Grammar Section 21.4.

It's a public holiday today.
There's no one in the office.
See Business Grammar Section 8 for notes on the use of articles (*a*, *the*, and when no article is needed).

Could you tell her that Rosa called?
Could you ask her to call me?
You can also use *say*.
Could you say (that) Rosa phoned? (not *Could you say her that Rosa …*)
See Business Grammar Section 17.10 for more on *say*, *tell* and *ask*.

Do you have any time this afternoon?
No, but I have some free time tomorrow.
See Business Grammar Section 10.1 for examples of *some* and *any*.

Have we covered everything?
Thanks (thank you) for calling.
Note these ways of bringing a call to an end.

I sometimes have problems on the phone.
Discussing your English skills:
I need to improve my written/spoken English.
It's difficult to understand some accents.
I can manage well in every day situations.

Practice

Authentic listening

1 The speakers are talking about using English in their work. Answer the questions.

a How much does the Swedish financial controller use English at work?
When does she have problems with English?

b When does the Chilean clerk need English?
When does he have problems?

Short telephone conversations

2 Fill in the gaps using phrases from the box. Then listen and check your answers.

got a minute	Go ahead
three o'clock your time	tell him I called
to you later	give him the message
Is that	we covered everything
Are you busy?	

1 **A:** Hello. **a** .... Tarmo?
B: Speaking.
A: Hello, Tarmo. It's Teresa Milo here. Have you **b** .... ?
B: Hi Teresa. Yes, sure. **c** ....
A: It's about Thursday's meeting. I need to ...

2 **A:** Esther Briggs.
B: Esther. Hi! It's Maurice Penn here. **d** .... ?
A: Yes, I'm in a meeting at the moment. Can I call you back this afternoon? About **e** ....
B: Yes, of course. Speak **f** ....

3 **A:** Is there anything else? Have **g** .... ?
B: Just one thing. Could you ask Helmut to call me? Could you **h** .... ?
A: Sure. I'll **i** ....

Articles: a/an, the/-

3 What are the differences in meaning between the two alternatives?

e.g. I read the paper / the papers on the train this morning.
'the paper' = the newspaper
'the papers' = documents or newspapers

a Do you know Amir Khan / the Amir Khan?

....

b I left my briefcase in an office / the office.

....

c Did you go to hospital / the hospital on Sunday?

....

d I'd like a blue car / the blue car.

....

e The file is in a cupboard / the cupboard.

....

f Have you got time / any time this afternoon?

....

g Can you give him a message / the message?

....

Articles: a/an, the/-, some

4 Add *some*, *a/an* or *the* as necessary.

a When are we having .... lunch?
b I've got .... free time tomorrow.
c I'm going to .... Canary Islands in May.
d It's a public holiday today; it's .... Independence Day.
e We need to arrange .... time to meet.
f I'm calling about .... Thursday's meeting.
g I'm .... engineer by profession.
h Do you know .... time of the meeting?

UNIT 2

Developing contacts

Some useful phrases

Listen to the recording and repeat

Do you know any potential suppliers in the Poznan area?
There are a few I can recommend.
There are quite a lot.
Not very many.   Very few.
Do you have any other contacts in Poland?
Do you know anyone who supplies copiers?
Yes I do.   No, I'm afraid I don't.

We have a lot of contacts in Eastern Europe.
And I have a few very good contacts in Bulgaria.
I know several people who could help you.
I'm afraid we have very few contacts in that area.

What's your accountant like?
I can recommend her.
She's very efficient.
She's reliable and hard-working.
She's really good to work with.

Let me give you some other names and addresses.
I'll give you a letter of introduction.

AC is such a large company it's difficult to compete with it.
It's so efficient that we can't compete.

We met a couple of days ago.
last week   the week before last
Let's meet for lunch on the 10th.
in ten days' time   a week on Monday
I'll see you then.   I look forward to it.

Study notes

We have a lot of contacts in Eastern Europe.
I have a few very good contacts in Bulgaria.
I know several people who could help you.
I'm afraid we have very few contacts in that area.
Refer to usage of *much, many, a few, several,* etc. in Business Grammar Section 10.2.

She's very efficient.
She's reliable and hard-working.
Refer to a dictionary and check your knowledge of adjectives which can relate to different jobs:
an engineer: *clever, competent, hardworking,* etc.
a salesman: *outgoing, self-confident, persuasive,* etc.
Note that two-part adjectives are often hyphenated (*hard-working*), while some become one word (*outgoing*).

AC is such a large company it's difficult to compete with it.
It's so efficient that we can't compete.
For notes on *so* and *such*, refer to Business Grammar Section 17.11.

We met a couple of days ago.
last week   the week before last
Some other expressions referring to past time:
It was last Tuesday.   *It was two months ago.*
the Monday before last   *two weekends ago*

Let's meet for lunch on the 10th.
Other time expressions of referring to the future:
Are you OK for next Friday?   *What about this Friday?*
I prefer the Friday after next!
See Business Grammar Section 13.1 for notes on expressions of time.

in ten days' time
Some examples of time phrases:
I'll see you at 4 o'clock/at lunchtime   *in the morning/in the spring*
on the 27th/on your birthday   *this Thursday/next week.*

Practice

Contacts abroad

1 Listen to Lisa Little, an export sales co-ordinator, as she talks about her contacts. Are the statements true [T] or false [F]?

a Lisa has very little to do with production people in the factory. ☐
b Customers frequently call her direct. ☐
c The company has five agents worldwide. ☐
d There are some problems with the Portuguese agent. ☐
e Lisa has no communication problems. ☐

much, many *and* a lot (of)
(a) few, (a) little, several
so *and* such (a)

2 Choose the correct word.

e.g. I have a few (few/little) contacts in the tourism business.

a The order was .... (so / such) big that we couldn't handle it on our own.
b I know very .... (few / little) people who could help you.
c We don't sell very .... (a lot / much) in Turkey.
d They have .... (so / such) good contacts that it's difficult to compete with them.
e Are there .... (many / much) more calls to make?
f We have very .... (few / little) time.
g I can recommend him, because he's .... (so / such) reliable and hard-working.
h I know .... (few / little) people who are so efficient.

Adjectives describing personal qualities

3 Complete the sentences with a form of the word in brackets.

e.g. You can ask her. She's very helpful. (help)

a He is .... and very .... (rely; hard / work)
b She is very .... (efficiency)
c We need someone who is .... (energy)
d Everyone likes him; he's very .... (like)
e She has always been .... to me. (friend)
f He's good at his job, and .... (high / qualify)
g She has a lot of friends. She's warm and .... (out / go)
h He's a good worker, ... and .... (cheer, competence)

Time differences

4 Put the telephone dialogue in order.

e.g. **e** Hello.
f Hello. Yes?
b Can I speak to Carla Vito, please?

a And it's Labor Day. Nobody works today.
b Can I speak to Carla Vito, please?
c Carla Vito. That's V-I-T-O.
d Excuse me, but do you know what the time is?
e Hello.
f Hello? Yes?
g OK, I'll be in touch tomorrow. Sorry to disturb you.
h It's four o'clock in the morning.
i Am I too late? Is the office closed?
j Oh. I thought you were six hours behind us.
k Who? What was the name?

Practice

Time references

5 Use the time reference in the box to complete the sentences.

Today is Wednesday, 3 March 2010.

next month	in three months' time
a couple of months ago	the day before yesterday
last August	a week on Friday
in a fortnight / in two weeks	the month after next
three months ago	eighteen months ago
last year	a week tomorrow
the other day	

a A meeting in September 2008 took place ....

b A meeting in December took place ....

c A meeting in January took place ....

d A meeting on 17 March will take place ....

e A meeting in June will take place ....

f A meeting late in February took place ....

g .... was 2009.

h .... is April.

i May is ....

j August 2009 was ....

k 11 March is ....

l 1 March was ....

m Next week, on Friday, is ....

Making use of contacts

6 Write the questions for these answers.

e.g. – Do you have any contacts in Vietnam/Cambodia?
– Yes. I have a lot of contacts in that area.

a – Do you know ....?
– Yes. Let me give you some names and addresses.

b – Who can .... ?
– I can recommend several people we use.

c – Can you give .... ?
– Impex SA, for example, could help you.

d – What are .... ?
– They're very reliable and efficient. We use them a lot.

e – How can I .... ?
– I'll give you a letter of introduction.

f – There are some other things I'd like to talk to you about.
– Can we arrange .... ?
– Let's see. What about lunch next week?

UNIT 3

Out of the office

Some useful phrases

Listen to the recording and repeat

I'm trying to contact Toria Noritz.
Do you know how I can get in touch with her?
Is it possible to contact her on this number?
Where can I get hold of her?

I'm meeting Saleh this evening.
We're going out to dinner.
Do you have his number?

I'm afraid the office is closed.
He has already gone home.
I'm afraid we don't give out private numbers.

Shall I ask him to call you in the morning?
Would you like me to get a message to him?
Let me get him to call you.

Would you ask him to phone me, please?
Could you give him a message?
Yes, of course.
Would you mind calling back tomorrow?
No problem.

I've been trying to contact you.
I didn't know how to reach you.
Your mobile was switched off.

It's good to see you again.
It's good to be here.
I'm glad you made it.

This is a message for Fiona.
Hi, it's Peter. It's about next Friday.
I'll be on my mobile all afternoon.
I'll try and call you again later.

Study notes

I'm trying to contact Toria Noritz.
Where can I get hold of her?
Some other expressions when you need to contact someone:
Have you seen Toria today?
Has Toria arrived yet?
Will she be in this afternoon?

I'm afraid we don't give out private numbers.
Note the use of *I'm afraid* or *I'm sorry* to soften a negative message:
I'm afraid she's not at her desk.
I'm afraid I don't have her mobile number.
I'm sorry, but she has gone home.

Shall I ask him to call you in the morning?
Would you like me to get a message to him?
See Business Grammar Section 18.2 for more examples of offers.

Would you ask him to phone me, please?
Could you give him a message?
See Business Grammar Section 18.1 for more examples of requests.

Would you mind calling back tomorrow?
No problem.
Note other possible replies to *Would you mind ...?*:
No, not at all. *Of course not.*
See Business Grammar Section 18.1.

Your mobile was switched off. (US pronunciation)
I'll be on my mobile ... (UK pronunciation)

This is a message for Fiona.
Hi, it's Peter. It's about next Friday.
Some typical examples of voicemail messages. Note also:
Hi Sauli, If you get this message, please call me ...
Let me know that you received this.
I'll be on my mobile if you need me.

Practice

Leaving a phone message

1 Listen and fill in the form.

MESSAGE

MESSAGE TO: ....

TIME: .... **DATE:** ....

FROM: ....

PHONE No: ....

MOBILE No: ....

MESSAGE: ....

Trying to make contact

2 Listen to the recordings and answer the questions.

a Where is Pedro Ramez?
What time is it in Spain?
What is Viktor Tomasov's message?

b What did Viktor Tomasov want to talk about?
What does Pedro ask Viktor to do?
What is the time difference between Spain and Russia?

Telephone terms

3 Match the two parts of the sentences.

a	Do you know how I can get	**i**	my voicemail.
b	Would you like me to get	**ii**	how to reach you.
c	Would you mind not	**iii**	in touch with him?
d	I have been trying	**iv**	I got a message to call you.
e	We didn't know	**v**	him to ring you in the morning?
f	Who covers for you	**vi**	to contact you.
g	Leave a message on	**vii**	while you are away?
h	I'm ringing because	**viii**	calling me tomorrow?

4 Write these requests and offers in another way.

e.g. Why don't we meet again tomorrow?
Let's meet again tomorrow.

a Could we postpone the meeting until next week?
....

b Would you mind not opening the window?
....

c Let's have lunch out on Monday week.
....

d Would you call the HR department for me please?
....

e Shall I get him to ring you?
....

f Please don't tell him I called.
....

g Let me get her to call you in the morning.
....

h Can I get you a coffee?
....

Prepositions

5 Complete the sentences with an appropriate preposition where necessary.

e.g. I tried to get hold ...of... you yesterday.

a Your mobile was switched ....
b Your switchboard seems to close .... very early.
c How can I get .... touch .... your boss?
d I left a message .... your voicemail.
e Do you have anything to do .... the PR department?
f I'd like to introduce you .... Karol.
g We do a lot of business .... India and Pakistan.
h We deal mainly .... carpets.
i We are agents .... a large Turkish company.

UNIT 4

Introducing your company

Some useful phrases

Listen to the recording and repeat

What type of company is it?
It's a public limited company.
They make electronic sensors.
They're in the export business.

The company has three divisions.
Tommy Hoe is the chief accountant.
He reports to the finance director.
Tommy has a staff of 12.

My company is based in Sweden.
We're on the east coast.
Our head office isn't far from Stockholm.

Our main European factory is about 70 kilometres east of Brussels.
It's outside a place called Bruges.
It's just off the ring road.
It will take you two hours to drive there.

Excuse me, where is the main office?
Can you tell me how to get to the warehouse?

The warehouse is behind the administration block.
The training department is on the third floor.
My office is on the other side of the building.
It's at the end of the corridor.
If you get lost, just ask someone!

Our annual turnover is approximately $2.5 million.
Their sales are just over €3.5 million.
In comparison, Nabiko's worldwide sales are over ¥1.2 billion.

Study notes

It's a public limited company.
A public limited company (plc) = a company in which shares can be bought by the public. See the glossary of business-related terms (page 118) for definitions of other business organisations – *partnership, sole trader, proprietor.*

He reports to the finance director.
Tommy has a staff of 12.
Note also:
The finance director is his boss. *Twelve people work for him.*
Twelve people report to him.

We're on the east coast.
The training department is on the third floor.
It's at the end of the corridor.
See Business Grammar Section 13.2 for examples of prepositions of place.

Our main European factory is about 70 kilometres east of Brussels.
Some other examples of describing geographical position:
Our office is to the north-east of Cairo.
We are two kilometres west of Oslo.
Our office is in the southern part of the city.

It will take you two hours to drive there.
Helping with directions:
I'll send you a map. *It's easy to find.* *You can't miss it.*

Excuse me, where is the main office?
Can you tell me how to get to the warehouse?
Other ways to ask for directions on company premises:
What's the best way to …? *Can you direct me to …?*

Our annual turnover is approximately $2.5 million.
Nabiko's worldwide sales are over ¥1.2 billion.
See Business Grammar Section 21.1 for examples of high numbers.

Practice

Authentic listening

1 Listen, and fill in the missing words in the passages below.

a Our company **i** .... interior designers. It has **ii** .... , and was the first architectural practice to be quoted on the London Stock Exchange. Our current turnover **iii** .... Our head office **iv** .... Berlin and Dubai. Our principal work is **iv** ....
....

b **i** .... is to produce materials-handling equipment in the form of fork-lift trucks. Throughout the world, **ii**..............
....
....
In the UK **iii** ....
making fork-lift trucks – one concentrating on electric trucks and the other on engine-driven trucks.

Company details

2 Listen to the exchange, then number the words below 1–9 in the order in which you hear them.

acquisitions	☐	sale	☐
business	☐	subsidiaries	☐
clients	☐	supplier	1
employees	☐	turnover	☐
profit	☐		

High numbers

3 From the table below, write the numbers in full.

e.g. The area of Venezuela is....point nine one million square kilometres .

a The area of Brazil ....

b It's population ....

c Argentina's population ....

d Colombia's area ....

e The population of Peru ....

f Chile's population ....

g The area of Argentina ....

h The population of Colombia ....

	Population (m)	Area (sq km)
Argentina	39.53	2.78
Brazil	186.2	8.51
Chile	15.9	.75
Colombia	42.9	1.14
Peru	27.9	1.29
Venezuela	25.3	.91

From *The World Factbook*

Practice

Background information

4 Write questions using the words given. Then write answers to them with reference to your own experience.

e.g. Where / company / located?

Where is the company located?

It is located in San Francisco.

a What / type / company?

....

....

b What / main activities?

....

....

c Where / main markets?

....

....

d How / company organised?

....

....

e What / job title / your boss?

....

....

f Who / he (she) / report to?

....

....

g How many / employees / company?

....

....

h Where / company / based?

....

....

Directions and prepositions

5 Complete the sentences with suitable prepositions. Then write directions to your office or site.

e.g. I live ...in... the northern part of the city.

a To get .... our office, take the exit at junction 19.

b Turn left .... the traffic lights.

c Follow the signs .... Valletta.

d Our offices are .... a commercial area.

e We are right .... the main road.

f I live .... the suburbs.

g My house is not far .... the station.

h To get to my house, take the road .... the airport.

i My road is the third turning .... the left.

j The house is surrounded .... trees.

UNIT 5

Company profiles

Some useful phrases

Listen to the recording and repeat

I work for a power company.
I believe it's state owned.
I think it's publicly owned.
It's a public utility company.

Does the company receive subsidies?
Is it subsidised?
It receives substantial government subsidies.
Although it's a state monopoly, it's run like a private company.

What are your main business activities?
Where are your main sites?
How many people do you employ?
Where are your main markets?

Basically, we make and distribute electricity.
We operate a number of power stations.
gas works — water works
sewage plants — coal mines
We are the world's largest producer of electricity.
We account for 94% of the electricity produced in the country.

I believe we are the largest producer of gas in the region.
We are the market leaders.

And what do you do in the company?
What's your job? What's your position?
I'm an engineer, but I work as a project manager.
Currently, I'm working in Algeria.

MBV do a lot of business with gas companies.
They make very good profits.

Study notes

I believe it's state owned.
I think it's publicly owned.
Note that verbs such as *believe, think, want* and *feel* are actually used in the simple form. We do not say:
I am believing that …
See Business Grammar Section 1.1.

It's a public utility company
A 'utility' company is a company that supplies electricity, gas, water, etc. A 'public' utility company is one that is owned by the state. Alternatively, a company can be 'privately' owned.

It's run like a private company.
I work as a project manager.
See Business Grammar Section 17.5 for notes on the use of *as* and *like*.

Does the company receive subsidies?
Is it subsidised?
Note the use of *subsidy/subsidise*.
Other examples:
The company is heavily subsidised. *We receive no subsidies.*

We account for 94% of the electricity produced in the country.
Note this use of *account for*: *Who accounts for the rest?*
In this example, to *account for* = be responsible for/to produce.

I'm an engineer, but I work as a project manager.
Currently, I'm working in Algeria.
For more examples of the Simple Present tense vs. Continuous Present tense, see Business Grammar Section 1.1.

MBV do a lot of business with gas companies.
They make very good profits.
There are further examples of *do* and *make* in Business Grammar Section 17.7.

Practice

Authentic listening

1 Listen to the two speakers and choose the best answers.

Speaker 1

a How many offices has the business got?

- **i** two ☐ **ii** three ☐
- **iii** four ☐ **iv** five ☐

b How many categories of business does he talk about?

- **i** two ☐ **ii** three ☐
- **iii** four ☐ **iv** five ☐

c In general, what type of business is it?

- **i** security ☐ **ii** manufacturing ☐
- **iii** finance ☐ **iv** building ☐

Speaker 2

d How many people are involved in the partnership?

- **i** two ☐ **ii** four ☐
- **iii** more than four ☐ **iv** unspecified ☐

e How many support departments does he mention?

- **i** none ☐ **ii** two to four ☐
- **iii** more than four ☐ **iv** unspecified ☐

An overview of a stationery company

2 Listen to the sales director of a company which manufactures stationery products. Then complete the sentences.

e.g. Our company employs ......160 people...... .

a We operate on a site of

....

b We are approximately five miles

....

c The site which we operate from is a

....

d We have been here for

....

e Last year we had a turnover of

....

f This turnover is split between

....

g and items which we manufacture under

....

h We have a small amount of

....

i Our customers include

....

j from primary schools through

....

A short company profile

3 Fill in the gaps using words from the box.

as ✓	competition	exclusive
general	government	law
like	majority	market
monopoly	public	shares
shareholders	state-owned ✓	

Sucosa was founded **a** ....as.... a **b** ....state-owned....
c ...., but in 2004, 49% of its
d .... were sold on the open
e .... At the same time the
f .... was changed to permit
g .... but Sucosa continues to have an **h** .... contract to supply the military and other **i** .... agencies. **j** .... all companies, it holds an annual **k** .... meeting for its **l** .... but in its case the
m .... shareholder is the
n ....

Practice

Uses of make *and* do

4 Write the correct form of *make* or *do* in these sentences.

a We need it by 5pm. Please .... your best.

b We are still .... a lot of business with Taiwan.

c Did you .... a profit on the deal?

d I've got a lot of work to .... today.

e Another customer has .... a complaint about the AB2 range.

f Could you .... me a favour?

g Could you .... the meeting 3 o'clock, not 3.30?

h We are .... good progress at the moment.

i The company .... compressors for refrigerators.

j He's prepared to sell; .... him an offer.

k We have .... very well in the last six months.

Simple Present vs. Present Continuous

5 Write the verb in brackets in either the Simple Present or Present Continuous tense. In some cases there is more than one possibility.

e.g. I ...see... (see) your company is ...doing... (do) very well at the moment.

a I .... (still, work) on the BW project.

b BW .... (own) a lot of land in Canada.

c We .... (invest) very heavily in robotics.

d I .... (not, think) I told you about it.

e It .... (take up) nearly all my time.

f I .... (go) to Canada every month or so.

g I .... (usually, fly) Air Canada.

h But Iberia .... (do) a special offer for this month only.

UNIT 6

Competitors

Some useful phrases

Listen to the recording and repeat

We specialise in mail order.
We're more profitable than our competitors.
We're the most profitable company in Italy.
Our competitors are far less profitable.
Their prices are higher.
They have fewer customers than us.

We offer a better service than our competitors.
The quality of our products is far higher.
Our sales network is much better.
In my view, price is the most important factor.
What is the least important factor?

What's your opinion? What do you think?
I think that the location of a business is vital.
I agree. I don't agree.
I don't think that's true.
Customers want the best quality at the cheapest price.

We consider ourselves to be the best in the business.
We're one of the largest producers in Asia.
We rank in the top ten companies worldwide.
We have a very strong market position.

The competition in our business is very hard.
We face tough competition.
The European market is so difficult that we can't compete.
We need to be more competitive.

We can't compete on price.
Our competitors' wage costs are lower.
Their supply chain is more streamlined.

Study notes

We're more profitable than our competitors.
We're the most profitable company in Italy.
Note how we can use intensifiers with comparative and superlative adjectives:
We are much more profitable than … *We are by far the most effective …*
See Business Grammar Sections 11.3 and 11.5.

Our competitors are far less profitable.
What is the least important factor?
Note how we can also make comparisons expressing equality:
They are just as profitable as we are. *They are the same as us.* etc.

What's your opinion? What do you think?
Note these expressions for giving opinions and for agreeing/disagreeing:
I think …
I agree. *I agree with you.*
I don't think that's true.
I disagree.
Also note:
In my opinion … / In the CEO's opinion … (formal)
I reckon / I guess / I figure (informal)
I'm not sure / I'm not convinced that …
See Business Grammar Section 18.6.

We're one of the largest producers in Asia.
The European market is so difficult that we can't compete.
See Business Grammar Section 21.5 for notes on geographical locations.

The competition in our business is very hard.
We face tough competition.
Some other adjectives for describing competition:
fierce competition *(un)fair competition* *weak competition*

Their supply chain is more streamlined.
The *supply chain* is the network created by companies for producing, handling, distributing and selling their products.

Practice

Authentic listening

1 Number the ideas (1–3) in the order that you hear them.

a **An English production director**

- **i** They are maintaining their market share. ☐
- **ii** They have very firmly established markets, especially in Europe. ☐
- **iii** In this industry there is very intense competition. ☐

b **An English consulting engineer**

- **i** In the domestic market, price dominates. ☐
- **ii** For international work, their reputation is more important than the price. ☐
- **iii** There are too many firms chasing too little work. ☐

Comparing companies

2 Listen to a comparison of two industrial plants. Tick the best answer to each question.

a How does the Chilean plant compare in costs?

- **i** much more expensive ☐ **ii** about the same ☐
- **iii** a bit more expensive ☐ **iv** less expensive ☐

b How does the Chilean plant compare in size?

- **i** much larger ☐ **ii** about the same ☐
- **iii** a bit larger ☐ **iv** smaller ☐

c How does it compare in profitability?

- **i** much more profitable ☐ **ii** about the same ☐
- **iii** a bit more profitable ☐ **iv** less profitable ☐

d How does it compare in age?

- **i** much more modern ☐ **ii** about the same ☐
- **iii** a bit more modern ☐ **iv** less modern ☐

Practice

Asking opinions

3 Write questions asking for an opinion, using the words given.

e.g. What / think / this?
What do you think about/of this?

a What / opinion / sales results?
....

b agree / your colleague / this?
....

c What / view / product?
....

d consider / this / good / investment?
....

e Who / think / replace / chairperson / Kazoloo?
....

f In / opinion / product / good / quality?
....

g Why / think / Brazil / good / market?
....

Comparatives and superlatives

4 Put the words in brackets in comparative or superlative form. Sometimes both forms are possible.

e.g. The new model is the ....safest.... (safe) ever made, and it is also ..less noisy.. (little / noisy) than the .....older..... (old) one.

a Our .... (large) competitor is ten or twelve times .... (big) than us, but they are not our .... (dangerous) competitor; they are the .... (little / important) to us.

b What worries us .... (much) is the .... (small) companies, who are .... (flexible) and .... (quick) to react.

c The .... (important) thing now is to be flexible. The .... (fast) your reaction is, the .... (happy) your customers are.

Building vocabulary

5 Put the word in brackets in the correct form.

e.g. (compete) The price is not very ..competitive.. .

a (profit) This line is less .... these days.

b (special) We are .... in doing business in Eastern Europe.

c (compete) Is there much .... in your field?

d (produce) They're the largest .... of steel in the region.

e (invest) The new plant is an .... of some importance.

f (produce) Our .... are all high quality.

g (compete) All our .... beat us on price.

h (produce) Our full .... capacity is 60,000 units a month.

UNIT 7

Your personal background

Some useful phrases

Listen to the recording and repeat

I was born in the south of Spain.
Where do you live now?
In a small village 20 kilometres from Madrid.
We have a house in the middle of the village.
It's a terraced house.
How long have you lived there?

Are you married?
Do you have any children?
Yes, I have three children. Two boys and a girl.
They're still at school.
My daughter is the oldest. She's 14.

What are you doing these days?
Are you still in the food industry?
Yes, but I'm not working full time.
I work part time.

Do you still work for Danilo?
Hasn't he retired yet?
Have you ever been self-employed?
Have you ever had to cancel a holiday?
Have you ever had to fire someone?
No, never. Yes, but it was a long time ago.

What do you do in your free time?
I spend most of my time gardening.
I prefer being outside.
I'm not very keen on watching TV.

How have you been recently?
Very well.
I've had a bad back. I've been off work.
I've been in hospital.
I'm sorry to hear that.

Study notes

I was born in the south of Spain.
Note *I was born* (not *I am born*) *in Spain.*

It's a terraced house.
Other types of housing include:
a detached house a bungalow
a flat/apartment a maisonette.

Are you married?
Note also:
I'm single/divorced/separated.
Do you have a boyfriend/girlfriend/partner?
How long have you been together?
Note that a *partner* describes a long-term non-specific relationship.

Do you still work for Danilo?
Hasn't he retired yet?
See Business Grammar Section 17.13 for uses of *still* and *yet*.

Have you ever been self-employed?
How have you been recently?
I've had a bad back.
For examples of the Present Perfect tense, see Business Grammar Section 1.3.

Have you ever had to cancel a holiday?
See Business Grammar Section 7.3 for use of *have to*, and similarities and contrasts with the use of *must*.

Have you ever had to fire someone?
Yes, but it was a long time ago.
See Business Grammar Section 1.2 to revise the use of the Present Perfect and Past Simple tenses.

I'm sorry to hear that.
Some other expressions of sympathy:
That's terrible. *What a shame.* *Please pass on my best wishes.*
Hope you get well soon.

Practice

Authentic listening

1 Listen to the three speakers and answer the questions.

Speaker 1

a Where does he come from?
b How long has he been in Britain?
c Approximately how old are his children?

Speaker 2

d Where does he come from?
e What does his wife do?
f What gender are his children?

Speaker 3

g Where does she come from?
h What age and gender are her children?

Leisure interests

2 Listen and tick the things which the speaker has done in the last month. Then answer the questions for yourself.

In the last month	has the speaker	have you
watched TV?	☐	☐
read a book?	☐	☐
done any gardening?	☐	☐
had friends round for a meal?	☐	☐
been to a restaurant?	☐	☐
done any DIY (do-it-yourself)?	☐	☐
been to exercise classes?	☐	☐
been to the cinema?	☐	☐
been to a nightclub?	☐	☐
been to a sports club?	☐	☐
been away on holiday?	☐	☐
been to the theatre?	☐	☐
been to the zoo?	☐	☐
other	☐	☐

have to vs. had to

3 Write the correct form of *have, have (to), had, had (to)*, as appropriate.

e.g. It's a monopoly, so they ....have.... never ....had to.... worry about competition.

a We'll .... work overtime next week.

b – We still .... told the workers about the new schedule.
– Do we .... tell them now?

c In my first job, we .... start at seven.

d We .... not .... as bad a time as some of our competitors.

e My father-in-law is 66, but he .... retire yet.

f .... you ever .... cancel a holiday?

g My family were poor, and we .... be very careful with money.

h I .... never .... fire someone.

Vocabulary

4 Write four terms in each category. Include examples that are relevant to you.

a Accommodation: e.g. ....apartment....
b Health: ....asthma....
c Interests: ....reading....
d Occupation: ....clerical worker....

Practice

still, yet *and* again

5 Complete the sentences with *still*, *yet* or *again*.

e.g. Have the Penang office contacted you ...yet... ?

a My children are .... at school.

b What are you doing these days? Are you .... in the travel business?

c My children are quite young. They're not working ....

d Do you .... work for DBS?

e It's nice to see you ....

f I'm .... working with Danilo.

g Danilo? Hasn't he retired .... ?

h We've been here an hour, and we're .... waiting.

Verb forms

6 Underline the correct verb forms. Sometimes both options are correct.

a I **i** am born / **ii** was born in the south of Spain.

b How long **i** are you / **ii** have you been self-employed?

c **i** Did you / **ii** Have you ever had to fire someone?

d How **i** are your family? / **ii** have your family been?

e **i** Do you still work / **ii** Are you still working for the government?

f He doesn't agree with the new policies, so he **i** is resigned. / **ii** has resigned.

g I **i** am / **ii** have been in Sales all my life.

h The situation **i** hasn't changed / **ii** didn't change much since yesterday.

UNIT 8

Conditions of work

Some useful phrases

Listen to the recording and repeat

What benefits do you receive in your job?
Do you get private health insurance?
Does your company pay your phone bill?
Is there a bonus scheme?
What's the scheme worth?

What's your office like?
Is it a good place to work?
Is it noisy? Is it a friendly place?
Is there enough space for everyone?
Is the lighting bright enough?

There's plenty of space.
The lighting is reasonable – it's not too bright.
The office chairs are very comfortable.
But the work surfaces aren't wide enough.
And some of the shelves are too high for me to reach.

Where were you working this time last year?
What were you working on?
I was working in Pisa on the Dexo project.

What were you doing between three and four o'clock this afternoon?
I was having a very late lunch.

I was making some coffee when the alarm went off.
When I got outside, smoke was coming out of the window.
I had just finished work.
I tried to call you, but you had already gone home.

Study notes

What benefits do you receive in your job?
Do you get private health insurance?
Some people have more benefits than others, such as:

a company car
a subsidised canteen
free phone calls
travel passes
a clothing allowance
use of a gym
a company pension scheme, etc.

The lighting is reasonable.
The office chairs are very comfortable.
Other factors which influence the quality of working life:
good central heating, air-conditioning, a friendly working atmosphere, a comfortable office environment, interesting colleagues, etc.

The work surfaces aren't wide enough.
The shelves are too high for me to reach.
See Business Grammar Section 17.15 for notes on *too* and *enough*.
Note the use of the preposition *for* in:
The workbench is too high for me to reach.
It's too heavy for him to carry.
etc.

Where were you working this time last year?
What were you working on?
I was making some coffee when the alarm went off.
For notes on the Past Continuous tense and its contrast with the Past Simple, see Business Grammar Section 1.4.

I had just finished work.
I tried to call you, but you had already gone home.
See Business Grammar Section 1.5 for notes on the Past Perfect tense and the contrast with the Past Simple.
I had is often contracted to *I'd* in everyday speech. See the notes on contractions in Business Grammar Section 21.7.

Practice

In the office building

1 Listen and match the speaker with the item he or she is talking about.

computer	speaker	
desk	speaker	
elevator/lift	speaker	
shelf	speaker	
seat	speaker	1

Past Perfect tense vs. Past Continuous tense

2 Put the verb in the Past Continuous (*was/were* + *-ing*) or Past Perfect (*had done*). Sometimes both forms are possible.

This time last year we **a** ...were working.... (work) overtime every weekend. People **b** .... (get) to work early; they **c** .... (leave) late; they **d** .... (work) through their lunch hour. Everyone **e** .... (try) extra hard. The previous year **f** .... (be) a difficult one. The company **g** .... (make) a loss that year, and we **h** .... (not, receive) any bonus. That was the first time that that **i** .... (happen) in years, and some people **j** .... (already, spend) the money before they realised. The boss said we **k** .... (do) enough to keep our existing customers happy, but not enough to get new ones. In our opinion, we **l** .... (not, do) too badly – our sales **m** .... (rise), when all our competitors' sales **n** .... (fall). But the boss **o** .... (look) for more effort. That was why we **p** .... (work) so hard.

Working conditions
enough/too

3 Rearrange the words to make sentences.

e.g. does firm offer health insurance private you your?
Does your firm offer you private health insurance?

a benefits do special receive what you?
.... ?

b bills company does pay phone your your?
.... ?

c bright enough for is lighting read the to you?
.... ?

d enough everyone for not workstations there to use were
....

e for high me reach shelves the to too were
....

f for many me remember there things to too were
....

Office equipment

4 Put the words into five categories, five words in each. Use a dictionary where necessary.

air-conditioning	cable ✓	carpet ✓
corridor	desk	filing cabinet
hard drive	elevator ✓	entrance
fan ✓	fuse	keyboard ✓
lamp	lift	mouse
plug	printer	radiator
screen	seat	shelves
socket	spotlight	stairs
switch	scanner	shredder

Category 1: ..Keyboard..........................
Category 2: ..cable..........................
Category 3: ..carpet..........................
Category 4: ..elevator..........................
Category 5: ..fan..........................

Practice

A recruitment agency advertisement

5 Read the advertisement for a secretarial recruitment agency. Then fill in the gaps with words from the box. Use a dictionary where necessary. Note that the style of the advert is rather ironic!

dictating	compose
correct	find
fixing	guarantee
let	provide
recruit	scrutinising
secure	use
waste	

Is your PA wasting your time?

- Time disappearing while you go through the whole Business Section of the *Times*, when really your PA should be **a** .... it for the articles that you need to see?
- Time spent **b** .... letters, which a competent PA would **c** .... for you?
- Time used up **d** .... important meetings which you are too nervous to **e** .... your PA fix?
- Time vanishing while you **f** .... unnecessary mistakes in second and third proofs? And all because you didn't **g** .... Maine-Tucker to find you a decent PA.

There is only one company to send out into the marketplace to **h** .... a quality PA, and that's Maine-Tucker. What's more we **i** .... every person we **j** .... for three months – a 100% refund guarantee for all three months!

We **k** .... 'top-drawer' PAs up and down the country and for companies abroad. There is only one proviso: we will only **l** .... the best. So why **m** .... any more time?

From Maine-Tucker

UNIT 9

Job descriptions

Some useful phrases

Listen to the recording and repeat

Kasha Meld is a qualified accountant.
She joined the company last year.
She trained as an accountant with Touche Ross.
Sanjay Patel studied law at university.
He also has a degree in business studies.

Maurice Pot is responsible for the day-to-day running of the department.
He has to liaise with the production manager.
He spends a lot of his time advising people.
He doesn't have much to do with the sales side of the business.

What's Kasha like?
She's honest and reliable.
dishonest unreliable
She's experienced and efficient.
inexperienced inefficient

What does Maurice look like?
He's quite tall. He has curly dark hair.
What's he wearing today?
He's wearing a pin-striped suit and a yellow spotted tie.
Kasha's wearing a light-coloured trouser suit.

Do you think I should wear a jacket and tie?
I don't need to wear a tie, do I?
No, you don't. It's a very informal occasion.
I need to wear something smart, don't I?
Yes, you do. It's going to be a formal dinner.

Study notes

Sanjay Patel studied law at university.
He also has a degree in business studies.
Some common qualifications:
Phd (*Doctor of Philosophy*)
MBA (*Master of Business Administration*)
MA (*Master of Arts*) *BSc* (*Bachelor of Science*)
Note that Sanjay has a degree *in* business studies. See Business Grammar Section 13.5 for other common verbs and related prepositions.

He has to liaise with the production manager.
Some other useful phrases:
She spends a lot of her time on …
He's responsible for the day-to-day running of the department.
He has a lot/nothing to do with marketing.

She's honest and reliable.
dishonest unreliable
Note these adjectives and their opposites. For a list of other common adjectives and opposites, see Business Grammar Section 11.2.

He's quite tall. He has curly dark hair.
He's wearing a pin-striped suit and a yellow spotted tie.
Kasha's wearing a light-coloured trouser suit.
Practise writing a short description of yourself. Use a dictionary if necessary. Imagine someone will be meeting you at the airport and you want to email them a description.

I don't need to wear a tie, do I?
I need to wear something smart, don't I?
Note the replies:
Yes, you do or *No you don't*. You could also say:
I think you should … or *I would/I wouldn't …*
See Business Grammar Section 15.2 for more on replying to negative statements. The more straightforward questions would be:
Do I need to wear a tie? *Is it formal or casual?* *What should I wear?*

Practice

Authentic listening

1 Listen, and fill in the charts.

a **An American administrative assistant**

Qualifications: A BA in Liberal Arts, Diploma in International Relations

Previous employment: ....

Current occupation: ....

b **An English production director**

Qualifications: ....

Previous employment: ....

Current occupation: ....

c **A Norwegian translator**

Qualifications: ....

Previous employment: ....

Current occupation: ....

Describing appearances and dress

2 Listen and match the descriptions with the people described.

Person 1 **Person 2** **Person 3** **Person 4**

a Person ☐

b Person ☐

c Person ☐

d Person ☐

Practice

Talking about responsibilities and experiences

3 Fill in the gaps with an appropriate word, if necessary.

e.g. He's the sales director, responsible ...for... the sales department.

a He handles .... the day-to-day running of the office.

b He has to liaise .... the production team.

c She trained .... an accountant .... Sydney University.

d He has a university degree .... management.

e She studied .... economics .... university.

f He doesn't have much to do .... our department.

g I wish I was qualified .... accountancy.

h I studied accountancy .... two years, but I'm not qualified .... an accountant.

Jobs/industries

4 Match the jobs (a–p) to the industries.

a accountant executive	accountancy
b steward	advertising
c chief cashier	airlines
d systems analyst	banking
e cook	car industry
f drug representative	civil engineering
g estate agent	computers
h machinist	hotel restaurant
i surveyor	insurance
j loss adjuster	mining
k quality controller	pharmaceuticals
l book-keeper	property
m editor	publishing
n pit manager	railways
o shop assistant	retail trade
p ticket inspector	textiles

Confirming statements

5 Confirm the statements.

e.g. It's not far away. ...No, it isn't....

We understand each other. ...Yes, we do....

a He graduated from Harvard. ....

b You don't agree with me, do you? ....

c She's not very well qualified. ....

d The job must come first. ....

e It wasn't important. ....

f They'd employ anyone. ....

g It's not been easy. ....

h They'd never met. ....

6 Read the text and answer the questions. Use a dictionary where necessary.

Sean Klein is an interpreter and translator with clients in advertising and commerce, media, transport and legal fields. Half Austrian by birth and brought up in a bilingual family, he still regards English as his mother tongue. He translates into English, and interprets in English, French and German.

He did a French and German degree at university followed by a course interpreting and translating.

He says: 'I have worked as a temporary translator for the UN and as a staff translator for Shell International, but I am now freelance. It takes a while to establish yourself. At first clients are more likely to give you translation work while you convince them of your linguistic ability. Now I do 40% interpreting and 60% translating.

'I do a lot of simultaneous work because I enjoy it. It is stressful and you have to think on your feet, but it is fantastically stimulating intellectually. I often breath a sigh of relief at the end of a successful conference – then return to the hotel to read paperwork for the next day.'

From *The Times*

a In which fields does Sean Klein specialise?

b Which is his first language?

c What did he study at university?

d Where did he work before going freelance?

e What is the ratio of interpreting to translating work?

f What does he often do at the end of a successful conference?

UNIT 10

Buying products

Some useful phrases

Listen to the recording and repeat

Our products are reasonably priced.
competitively priced   conveniently packaged
extremely well made   highly competitive

What are they made of?
The casing is made of plastic.
The working parts are all stainless steel.
The components are made in Spain.

The base is made of concrete.
Twenty-five per cent of the components are rubber.
Two-thirds of the parts are made of copper.
The structure covers 5 square metres.

We stock the full product range.
Most items are available from stock.
The XC range is currently out of stock.
When can you deliver the goods?
We offer next-day delivery.
Delivery usually takes two days.

How much do they cost?
How much are they?

The reference number is 12/473-AZ9.
I'd like to order one.
Do you still supply them in green?
I'm afraid we don't stock that colour anymore.
That line is discontinued.

We used to make them in that size.
We used to stock that design.
It used to be very popular, but there's no longer any demand for it.
What is the nearest equivalent?
The A444-909 is very similar.

Study notes

Our products are reasonably priced.
Note the use of adverbs in phrases as described in Business Grammar Section 12.4.

The working parts are all stainless steel.
Check the materials which you need to know in a dictionary.
Note collocations such as:
reinforced concrete   *windscreen glass*
rigid plastic   *locally sourced wood*, etc.

Twenty-five per cent of the components are rubber.
Two-thirds of the parts are made of copper.
Note that % is usually written *per cent* in UK English and *percent* in US English. For more on fractions and percentages, see Business Grammar Section 21.2.

The structure covers 5 square metres.
See Business Grammar Section 21.3 for notes on measurements in English.

Most items are available from stock.
The XC range is currently out of stock.
Some other expressions:
It's in stock.   *Stock levels are low.*
to do a stock take (to check the inventory)

How much do they cost? How much are they?
Some other phrases to do with prices:
Is that your best price?   *What does the price include?*
The price seems very high!

The reference number is 12/473-AZ9.
Note that the symbol / can be referred to as 'slash' or sometimes 'oblique'. It can be a forward slash or a back slash.
Z is pronounced /zii/ in US English and /zed/ in UK English.

We used to make them in that size.
We used to stock that design.
See Business Grammar Section 1.6 for notes on *used to*.

Practice

used to *and the verb* to use

1 Listen, and fill in the gaps. Then write similar examples based on your own experience.

a I **i** .... the fax machine all the time, but now I **ii** .... email. It's far more convenient.

b I **iii** .... an old PCs last week. I hadn't **iv** .... one for ages.

c I can't think of any products which we **v** .... All I can think of is people. We **vi** .... have a workforce of 32. Now we **vii** .... two robots, and we have a workforce of six.

d We installed a wireless system and for the last few years we have **viii** .... that.

Numbers and symbols

2 Listen and write down the numbers, dates and symbols which you hear.

a 23/09876-21B

b ....

c ....

d ....

e ....

f ....

g ....

h ....

i ....

Adverbs in phrases

3 Use the words in brackets to make phrases.

e.g. It is a (very / reasonable / price) very reasonably priced model.

a This is a (high / recommend) .... product.

b It is made out of (long / last) .... titanium.

c They are (extreme /attractive) .... and (good / make) .... goods.

d They are (very / wide / use) .... materials.

e This is a (high / competitive) .... offer.

f The cabinet is made of (special / select) .... wood.

g It is a (beautiful / design) .... piece.

h It is a (real / good / produce) .... unit.

A product enquiry

4 Complete the dialogue with the appropriate words/phrases from the box.

delivery	discontinued	in stock
line	manufacturers	order
out of stock	plastic	reference
stainless	stock	supply

A: I'd like to **a** .... some parts.

B: Certainly. Have you got a **b** .... number?

A: The number is C-302.

B: Is that made from **c** .... ?

A: No, the casing is **d** .... steel.

B: Those are **e** .... at the moment.

A: When do you expect a new **f** .... ?

B: There should be a **g** .... on Monday.

A: Have you got any of the C-202 **h** .... ?

B: The **i** .... have **j** .... that **k** .... but we may have some old **l** .... I'll see.

Practice

Materials

5 Match the materials and metals to their characteristics. Choose words from the box below. Add any other words which you can think of.

soft / hard	brittle / tough	strong / weak
flexible / rigid	heavy / light	flammable
man-made	edible	

a glass ......hard, brittle, rigid, etc.......

b paper ....

c iron ....

d PVC ....

e copper ....

f gold ....

g wood ....

h leather ....

i cotton ....

j nylon ....

k beef ....

Unusual products

6 Fill in the boxes in the illustration with the phrases listed. Use a dictionary as necessary.

BUGGING: HOW THE LISTENERS TAP IN

pen transmitter
briefcase with built-in recording equipment
desk calculator with built-in transmitter
plug adapter room transmitter
telephone transmitter
portable calculator transmitter
power socket transmitter

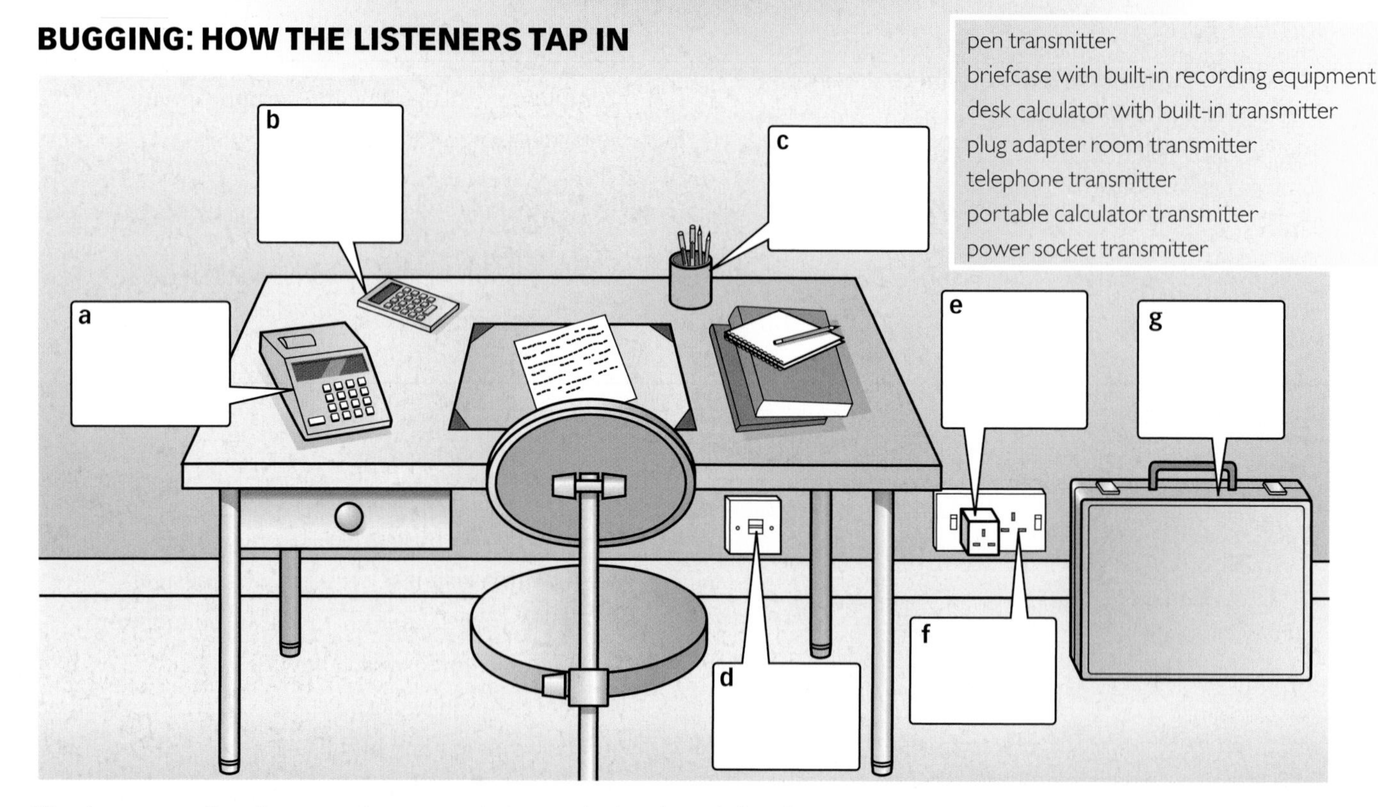

'They have ways of invading your privacy: many devices can be bought and placed in an office without the user ever knowing that their true purpose is eavesdropping.'

UNIT 11

Product descriptions

Some useful phrases

Listen to the recording and repeat

How long have you been making balloons?
For just over 20 years.
What about the 'P' series?
We've only been selling that model since the beginning of this year.

We're the largest manufacturer of balloons in the world.
On average, we build one every day.
No other manufacturer can match us.
These balloons range in size from 590 cubic metres to 2,550 cubic metres.
That's 90,000 cubic feet.

We also sell off-the-shelf packages.
All are available at the lowest possible prices.
They come in a range of colours and sizes.
There are various options.

Which different shapes are available?
Do you have any round ones?
This one is L-shaped.
That one is in the shape of a cross.

This is how they are made.
First, the fabric is cut into panels.
Then the panels are sewn together.
At this stage, the structure is reinforced.
Finally, it's connected to the frame.

Could you tell me if this is the latest version of the software?
Do you know whether it runs on this type of PC?
I'd like to know how often it needs updating.

Study notes

How long have you been making balloons?
We've only been selling that model since the beginning of this year.
See Business Grammar Section 1.3 for notes on the Present Perfect Continuous tense.

These balloons range in size from 590 cubic metres to 2,550 cubic metres.
That's 90,000 cubic feet.
Note the use of the comma (,) to indicate thousands in 90,000 and 2,550. In some countries a full stop (.) is used instead of a comma.
See Business Grammar Section 21.3 for notes on metric and imperial measurements.

Do you have any round ones?
This one is L-shaped.
Revise the words for standard shapes:
square, round, oval, rectangular, oblong, etc.
Most shapes can be described in terms of their resemblance to letters: *T-shaped, S-shaped*. They can also be described in terms of their resemblance to other objects: *barrel-shaped, star-shaped,* etc.

First, the fabric is cut into panels.
Then the panels are sewn together.
Finally, it's connected to the frame.
The Present Simple Passive tense is often used to describe processes. See Business Grammar Section 4.1.

Could you tell me if this is the latest version of the software?
Do you know whether it runs on this type of PC?
Examples of indirect questions which can give the effect of making the questions seem more polite. The direct questions for these examples are:
Is this the latest version? *Does it run on this type of PC?*
See Business Grammar Section 15.1 for more on indirect questions.

Practice

Authentic listening

1 Listen to the speakers describing processes in their industries. Complete the sentences, then number them in the order they take place.

a Manufacturing

i Individual components .... together. ☐

ii The truck .... and goes through final testing. ☐

iii Steel plate .... into shapes. ☐

b Fast-food catering

i .... across the counter. ☐

ii .... accurate measures of mustard and ketchup. ☐

iii .... the sesame seed bun in the toaster. ☐

Shapes

2 Listen, and match the descriptions which you hear with the objects.

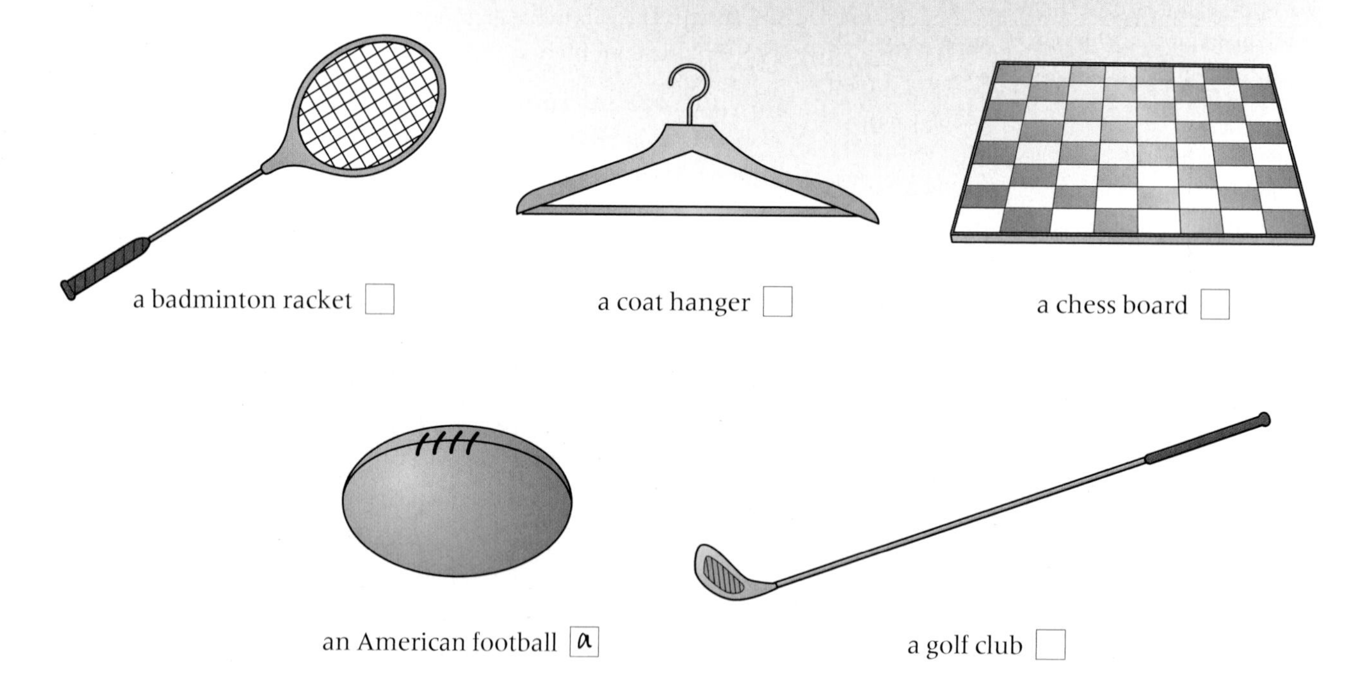

Practice

The Present Perfect vs. the Present Perfect Continuous

3 Put the verbs in either the Present Perfect (*have done*) or the Present Perfect Continuous (*have been doing*).

a I .... (never, see) that man before.

b How long .... (he, work) here?

c I .... (work) in the front office.

d I .... (not, notice) what .... (happen) in the factory.

e How many new people .... the company .... (hire)?

f I .... (lose) count of the number of interviews that they .... (do).

g They .... (not, stop) advertising even now.

h .... they .... (decide) to double the workforce?

Direct and indirect questions

4 Rewrite these sentences as direct questions.

e.g. Can you tell me what the P33 is like?
What is the P33 like?

a I'd like to know how much it costs.

....

b Can you tell me if this model is suitable for my needs?

....

c I'd like to know how often they need servicing.

....

d Do you know how long they have been producing this line?

....

e I'd be interested to hear why they changed the specifications.

....

f Can you tell me if you've got enough in stock?

....

g Do you know when you can deliver?

....

h I'd like to know if there's a discount for quantity.

....

The Simple Present Passive form

5 Rewrite the sentences using the Simple Present Passive.

e.g. They manufacture the panels in Belize.
The panels are manufactured in Belize.

a They make the crystals by freezing the liquid.

....

b They keep the mixture in a tank.

....

c They freeze it to −5°C.

....

d They constantly monitor the temperature.

....

e They leave it there for two hours.

....

f They take samples for analysis.

....

g They choose the smallest crystals.

....

h They throw away the larger ones.

....

UNIT 12

Faults and breakdowns

Some useful phrases

Listen to the recording and repeat

I would like to return ...
... some faulty, plastic smoke alarms.
... this lightweight graphite tennis racquet.
Some parts need replacing.
It needs sorting out.

The windows don't close properly.
The control system doesn't work.
There is something wrong with the case.
It's scratched.

broken	dented	cracked
faulty	damaged	substandard

We're very unhappy about the quality.
It isn't good enough.
I'm sorry to hear that.
We're very sorry.
We apologise for any inconvenience.
What can we do to put it right?

I spoke to the man who wrote the report.
I contacted the customer who made the complaint.
I'll phone the person whose job it is to mend it.

The customer was very pleased with the replacement.
He says it's been working very well indeed.
He hasn't had any more trouble with it.

That's good to hear.
Thank you for saying that.
I appreciate that.

Study notes

I would like to return ...
Note some other phrases when you need goods replaced or repaired:
I'm not happy about/with ... *I have a problem with ...*
The alarm you sold me doesn't work ...
If you need to be more formal:
I'd like to register a complaint about ...

some faulty, plastic smoke alarms
this lightweight graphite tennis racquet
Note these examples of adjectives used to describe products. Business Grammar Section 11.1 has guidelines on the order of adjectives.

Some parts need replacing. It needs sorting out.
Notice the use of the *-ing* form of the verb after *need*. See Business Grammar Section 6.2. The infinitive can also be used with *need*:
There are some things that need to be sorted out.
What needs to be replaced?

What can we do to put it right?
Some language for putting things right:
I'm sure we can sort it out. *We'll sort it out for you.*
We'll replace it. *We'll refund your money.*

I spoke to the man who wrote the report.
I contacted the customer who made the complaint.
Note you can also use *that* in these sentences (*the man that; the customer that*).

I'll phone the person whose job it is to mend it.
See Business Grammar Section 14.

That's good to hear.
Thank you for saying that.
I appreciate that.
Some useful phrases for responding to praise and compliments.

Practice

Authentic listening

1 Mark each statement true [T] or false [F] according to what the speakers say.

Speaker 1

- **a** The system generally is working well. ☐
- **b** There is a problem with the address function. ☐

Speaker 2

- **c** The speaker is generally happy with the product. ☐
- **d** The product doesn't work well in the bathroom. ☐

Speaker 3

- **e** The speaker is satisfied with the system. ☐
- **f** The instruction manual is difficult to understand. ☐

Order of adjectives

2 Put the words in order.

e.g. We have bought a ...high-quality laser... printer. (laser / printer / high-quality)

- **a** It's a .... (alarm / plastic / faulty / smoke)
- **b** It's a .... (company / mining / South African / large)
- **c** It was a .... (racket / new / fibre / tennis / glass)
- **d** We bought a .... (lamp / white / reading / ceramic)
- **e** It comes with a(n) .... (display / crystal / liquid / adjustable)
- **f** The market prefers .... (cheap / goods / imported / foreign)
- **g** The problem was a .... (component / hydraulic / defective)
- **h** We sell a(n) .... (system / security / new / electronic)

Causes for complaint, and prepositions

3 Complete the sentences with an appropriate preposition.

e.g. We are very unhappy ...about... the quality.

- **a** The car has broken .... again.
- **b** There is something wrong .... it.
- **c** It needs sorting ....
- **d** The lift is .... of order.
- **e** It is not .... good working order.
- **f** We've had a lot of trouble .... the motor. It's almost worn ....
- **g** We should complain .... the manufacturer .... it.
- **h** They should apologise .... the inconvenience.

Relative pronouns

4 Complete the sentences with an appropriate relative pronoun (*who, which, that, whose, where*). Sometimes nothing, or more than one, is possible.

e.g. This is the component ...that/which... caused all the problems.

- **a** That is the town .... the President was born.
- **b** It's the town .... he left when he was a young man.
- **c** They are people .... main interest is money.
- **d** It was our chief designer .... made the modifications.
- **e** I'll phone the person .... job it is to mend it.
- **f** The assembly is fitted with an electrical plug, in .... there is a 5-amp fuse.
- **g** All the machines .... we have recalled and inspected are perfectly safe.
- **h** There are no moving parts, ... means no maintenance.

UNIT 13

The services you provide and use

Some useful phrases

Listen to the recording and repeat

We do the office cleaning ourselves.
We handle our own cleaning.
We manage everything in-house.
We subcontract our logistics to CLK.
Routine maintenance work is done by an outside contractor.

CLK provides an excellent service.
The service they provide is very good value.

We ought to have our IT system updated.
We need to have all of our machines serviced.
We must get the job done soon.

We're considering whether to lease or to buy.
What's the cost of outright purchase?
What does it cost to lease?

There's a discount of 20% if you buy today.
There's a 20% discount.
The net price is $1,512.
Sales tax is extra.

The rental is €95 per day.
per week weekly
per month monthly

We offer a full service contract.
What does the contract include?
It covers routine and emergency call-outs.
It doesn't cover spare parts.
The service charge is $690 per annum.
The first six months are free of charge.

Study notes

We do the office cleaning ourselves.
We handle our own cleaning.
For notes on reflexive pronouns and the use of *own*, see Business Grammar Section 17.8.

We subcontract our logistics to CLK.
Other expressions relating to subcontracting:
We use a number of small subcontractors.
Maintenance of our heating systems is subcontracted.
Note also the use of *outsourcing*:
Many jobs in telephone sales have been outsourced.

We ought to have our IT system updated.
We need to have all of our machines serviced.
We must get the job done soon.
get appears to be a little less formal than *have*.
For notes on *have/get something done*, see Business Grammar Section 4.2.

We're considering whether to lease or to buy.
to lease = to rent/to hire
Note that a *lessor* (lesser, in US English) is the person who provides the product. The *lessee* is the person to whom the product is 'leased'.

There's a discount of 20% if you buy today.
discount can be used as a noun, verb or adjective:
They offered a good discount. (noun)
They have discounted their prices. (verb)
They sold it at a discount price. (adjective)

The rental is €95 per day.
Some other expressions to describe payment times and terms:
a quarterly charge *a yearly subscription* *an annual fee*
to make regular payments

Practice

Leasing vs. purchasing

1 Fill in the gaps using the words from the box. Then listen and check your answers.

buy	claim	company	expense
expenses	fleet	in-house	lease
leasing	outright	per	purchasing
repairs	tax		

To compare leasing with **a** .... , we can take the company car **b** .... as an example. We used to **c** .... all our cars **d** .... , but now we get them on a three-year **e** .... That way, our **f** .... are a fixed amount **g** .... month, so we can plan, and the leasing **h** .... is responsible for all the maintenance and **i** .... We used to handle that **j** .... before. In terms of **k** .... , if you're **l** .... you can **m** .... the total cost as a business **n** ....

Speakers talking about the help they receive

2 Listen and mark the following statements true [T] or false [F]. Then correct the false ones.

a The speaker has never had any help in the house. ☐

....

b The speaker employs a gardener. ☐

....

c The speaker does all the work. ☐

....

d The au pair only deals with the children. ☐

....

e The roof of the house needs repairing. ☐

....

to have/get something done

3 Rewrite the sentences, using *have/get (something) done,* to show someone else doing the action.

e.g. We ought to update the system.

We ought to have the system updated.

a We need to service the boilers.

....

b I have signed the contracts.

....

c Are you sorting everything out?

....

d We need to demolish and rebuild the whole factory.

....

e We sometimes did some market analysis.

....

f Shall I bring in some coffee?

....

g We didn't prepare a formal agreement.

....

h We took some photographs of the building.

....

Practice

Questions with need, must, have to, *etc.*

4 Write questions using the words given.

e.g. How far / he / have to / travel
How far does he have to travel ?

a How much / we / should / pay / them

.... ?

b Why / we / must / change / our suppliers

.... ?

c The rental / have to / pay / quarterly

.... ?

d How often / the machine / need / servicing

.... ?

e What /ought / service contract / include

.... ?

f Where / I / should / send / the bill

.... ?

g When /ought / the engineer / be / here

.... ?

h How much / we / need / pay /per month

.... ?

Reflexive pronouns

5 Complete the sentences with either *himself/herself,* etc., or *his own/her own,* etc.

e.g. They have to do everything themselves .

They have to do their own accounts.

a We have to do the cleaning ....

b He prefers to do it all .... these days.

c We handle .... cleaning.

d I do most of the marketing on ....

e Why don't you all type your letters .... ?

f The computer backs up the data by ....

g She makes .... decisions on sales.

h When I get a pilot's licence, I'll fly .... to important meetings!

UNIT 14

Service issues

Some useful phrases

Listen to the recording and repeat

We regret that we've had to cancel the course
... due to insufficient demand.
... because of financial difficulties.
... as a result of complaints by customers.

We've just heard that the delivery hasn't arrived.
As far as I know, they haven't received the goods yet.
It should have arrived by now.
We're very worried about the situation.

That's strange; it was despatched on Monday.
I've checked with the driver.
He says that he delivered it on Tuesday.
Apparently, Mr Carlos signed for it.

We apologise for any inconvenience which this might have caused.
We'd like to apologise for not delivering the goods on time.
Please accept our apologies.
We're very sorry about this.

Don't worry; it really doesn't matter.
Please don't apologise; it was no trouble.
There is really no need to apologise.
That's OK. No problem.

You really should have let us know sooner.
You ought to have made the situation clear.
You could have called us.

Study notes

We regret that we've had to cancel the course ...
We apologise for any inconvenience ...
Please accept our apologies.
Notice the range of ways in which we can apologise in English. All of these examples are formal and are more likely to be written than spoken:

due to insufficient demand
because of financial difficulties
as a result of complaints by customers
In terms of meaning, these terms can be used interchangeably:
The consignment was delayed due to the bad weather.
... because of the bad weather.
... as a result of the bad weather.
See also Business Grammar Section 16.1.

It should have arrived by now.
You really should have let us know sooner.
You ought to have made the situation clear.
See Business Grammar Section 7.1 for modal verb forms and specifically 7.7 for the Past tense of modal verbs used to express regret, criticism and unfulfilled expectation.

Apparently, Mr Carlos signed for it.
Apparently = From the information which I received.
Other examples:
Apparently, they have lost the invoice.
Apparently, they are out of stock.

Don't worry; it really doesn't matter.
Please don't apologise; it was no trouble.
Useful expressions for accepting apologies. See Business Grammar Section 18.4.

That's OK. No problem.
Informal way of accepting apologies.

Practice

Some complaints

1 Listen to the complaints. Then link each speaker to the appropriate business.

a	a bank	Speaker 3
b	an electrical service company	
c	a hotel	
d	a components supplier	
e	an international courier	

Late payment

2 Put the telephone conversation in the correct order.

A: I'd like to speak to Mr Diaz, please.

B: Diaz speaking.

A: ......

B: ......

A: ......

B: ......

A: ......

B: ......

A: ......

B: ......

A: ......

B: ......

A: ......

B: ......

A: ......

B: ......

A

i I'm sorry to hear that.
ii Then can we expect your payment today?
iii I'd like to speak to Mr Diaz, please.
iv I didn't know that. I'll talk to Mr Sanchez.
v Hello. This is Aminex here. It's about your account.
vi The terms of our agreement are payment not later than the third of the month.
vii It seems we haven't received your July payment yet.
viii Could you explain that, please?

B

a Yes. I know that.
b No, I'm afraid we're not paying this bill.
c He'll tell you all about it!
d I told Mr Sanchez. I said we were withholding payment until it was sorted out.
e No, that's right, you haven't.
f Diaz speaking.
g Your last delivery was very poor quality.
h What seems to be the problem?

Practice

due to, on account of, *etc.*

3 Rewrite the sentences using the phrases in brackets.

e.g. They don't want to invest since the current economic situation is bad.
(because of) They don't want to invest because of the current economic situation.

a We've had to cancel the course because the demand was insufficient.
(due to) ....

b The plane was diverted because there was fog in Lima.
(because of) ....

c We have cancelled the deal because we had problems with our suppliers.
(on account of) ....

d All flights are delayed as the weather is bad.
(due to) ....

e Since the government has introduced new regulations, we have changed our proposal.
(as a result of) ....

f Business has been good because the weather has been hot.
(on account of) ....

g Because customers have complained, we have had to recall that batch.
(as a result of) ....

h They have stopped making this line as the demand has been insufficient.
(due to) ....

The past of modal verbs

4 Complete the sentences with *should have, must have, could have, might have*. Sometimes there is more than one possibility.

a – Who left the lights on last night?
– It .... (be) John. He was the only person still here when I left.

b – Will it be delivered soon?
– Yes, it .... (arrive) by now.

c – I can't be here tomorrow.
– You .... (let) me know sooner. It's too late to make other arrangements now.

d – The heating engineer has made a complete mess of the system.
– We .... (ask) our own person to fix it.

e – I haven't received your CV yet.
– Oh dear, I think I .... (send) it to the wrong address.

f – I'm sorry I didn't get back to you last night. Your switchboard was closed.
– I was here. You .... (send) me a message.

g – Did you do anything about that policeman?
– No, We .... (make) a formal complaint, but we decided to forget it.

h – The client's a bit angry. What should I do?
– Write and say: 'We apologise for any inconvenience this .... (cause) you.'

UNIT 15

Service industries

Some useful phrases

Listen to the recording and repeat

Our company has more than 200 contracts in the south-west.
These range in size from small to very large.
We have some big customers such as KAZ and Mastor.

We'd like you to give us a quote.
How much do you charge for this kind of work?
Could you let us know your fees?
Can I check that your commission is still 1.5%?

Makara are specialists in recycling.
Companies pay a fixed price for a guaranteed supply of materials.
We hope to save more than 30% by using reconditioned pallets.

I hear that they have a combined turnover of £360 million.
Apparently, they employ 2,000 staff.
According to their sales people, the deal with Makara is worth $300 million.

They can't have said that.
They wouldn't have said that.
They must have meant $300,000.
You must have misunderstood.
They may have made a mistake.

The company has a strong ethical policy.
Price is not their main consideration when choosing a supplier.
They are very demanding.
They require a fast response if there are problems.

Study notes

We have some big customers such as ...
Other ways of providing examples:
We have some big customers – for example, Mastor.
Big customers, like Mastor, demand ...
Our customers include KAZ and Mastor.

We'd like you to give us a quote.
As an alternative to *quote*, we can use *estimate*.
Can you give us an estimate?
These words can also be used as verbs:
We'd like you to quote for the job.
We estimate it will cost €5,000!

Could you let us know your fees?
Can I check that your commission is still 1.5%?
Some useful expressions:
Our sales people work on a commission basis.
We charge a monthly fee.
Our fees are going up next year.

Makara are specialists in recycling.
Companies pay a fixed price for ...
Note the prepositions used. Here are some others:
We concentrate on the distribution side.
We rely on our suppliers.
We demand a fast response to our problems.

They can't have said that.
They wouldn't have said that.
They must have meant $300,000.
All of these phrases are useful when you need to correct misunderstandings. See Business Grammar Section 7 for notes on modal verbs.

Practice

Fees and charges

1 Listen to the three speakers, then mark what they are paid.

	Speaker a	Speaker b	Speaker c
an hourly rate		✓	
a fee			
expenses			
a commission			

Some company details

2 Listen, and complete the sentences.

a We now have over **i** .... , and we employ **ii** ....

b They range from small companies who want us to provide lunch for just a few people up to **iii** .... who require us to provide catering facilities **iv** ....

c They all have to go through a **v** .... , and all food handling staff have to pass an annual exam which tests **vi** ....

Prepositions

3 Complete the sentences with a suitable preposition.

e.g. It's different in a country like Uganda, ...for... example.

a They have some big customers .... India .... example.

b In an area like this, the customers vary a lot .... size.

c We hope to save more than 30% .... changing our systems.

d According .... the sales manager, the deal is worth a lot of money.

e They are specialists .... recycling materials.

f How much do you charge .... a job like this?

g We have to plan ahead .... next year.

h It's the same price as they quoted .... the last job.

A profile of an office servicing company

4 Using the words given, write a profile of an office servicing company.

e.g. service / more / 200 / clients / north-east.
We service more than 200 clients
in the north-east.

a specialise / interior design / offices

....

b clients / range / size / small / very large

....

c have / very large / clients / IBM / HP

....

d offer / complete service / design consultancy / supply / plants / flowers

....

e employ / 100 / full-time / part-time

....

f charge / fees / interior decoration / design

....

g customers / contracts / charge / monthly

....

h offer / important service / clients

....

Practice

Vocabulary

5 Complete the sentences with words from the box. Some of the words may be used twice.

charges	commission	charge	discount
fee ✓	price	quote	

a You're paying for the building materials, the labour costs and the architect's ....fee.... .

b Can you give me a .... for full insurance?

c When buying and selling shares for you, we charge a .... of 1%.

d My garage is too expensive. I must find one where the labour .... are more reasonable.

e Our salesmen get a 12% .... on everything they sell.

f Bank .... make up 1% of our costs.

g If we pay cash, we get a 5% ....

h The .... of the food includes tax and a service ....

Correcting misunderstandings

6 Correct the following misunderstandings using the words in brackets.

e.g. They said they had a combined turnover of £360 million.
(said/misunderstood) They can't have said that – you must have misunderstood.

a Apparently, they employ 20,000 staff – that's what they said.
(meant/meant 2,000) ....

b According to their sales people, the deal is worth $300 million to them.
(misunderstood/said $300 thousand) ....

c They may be expanding, but their PR person told me that they had fired 60 people last month.
(fired/meant hired) ....

d The marketing manager said she wants to cut the advertising budget by 15%.
(said that/made a mistake) ....

UNIT 16

Looking after visitors

Some useful phrases

Listen to the recording and repeat

Where do you usually take your foreign clients?
Do you ever take them sightseeing?
Not often. Very rarely.
We occasionally take them to the theatre.
We sometimes arrange a short boat trip for them.

Were you planning to do anything tomorrow night?
I was thinking of getting some tickets to the opera.
I was going to invite you out to dinner.
Would you rather go to a football match?
I'd prefer to go bowling.
I'm free every evening except Tuesday.

What should I wear tomorrow evening?
What's the dress code?
Should I bring a gift?

It's an informal occasion.
You needn't wear a suit.
You don't have to bring a gift, but I'm sure it would be appreciated.
We mustn't be late.

Always shake hands when you are introduced.
It's a good idea to carry your business cards.
It's best not to ask any personal questions.

Is there anything you don't eat?
Yes, I don't eat pork.
I can't have anything with sugar in it.
I'm vegetarian. I'm diabetic.
I'm on a diet. I'm allergic to seafood.
I love Lebanese food.

Study notes

Where do you usually take your foreign clients?
See Business Grammar Section 12 for notes on adverbs and specifically 12.5 for adverbs of frequency (*always, usually, often,* etc.).

Were you planning to do anything tomorrow night?
I was thinking of getting some tickets to the opera.
Note the use of *I was planning/thinking/wondering*, etc. to introduce tentative ideas and plans. See Business Grammar Section 1.7.

Would you rather go to a football match?
I'd prefer to go bowling.
would rather and *prefer* are alternative expressions. Both are followed by *than*:
I'd rather watch football than ice hockey.
I'd prefer to eat out than eat in.
See Business Grammar Section 17.17.

What should I wear tomorrow evening?
What's the dress code?
Some recommendations:
Wear something comfortable.
It's smart but casual.
I think it's a black tie dinner. (black tie = dinner jacket and bow tie)

You needn't wear a suit.
You don't have to bring a gift, but ...
We mustn't be late.
See Business Grammar Sections 7.4 and 7.5 for notes on *needn't* and *don't have to* compared with *mustn't*.

I can't have anything with sugar in it.
I'm allergic to seafood.
Some other food preferences:
I'm lactose intolerant.
I prefer not to eat red meat.
I don't drink alcohol.
I have a nut allergy.

Practice

Authentic listening

1 Match the speakers with the statement that best summarises their answer to the question: How do you entertain your business visitors?

a A marketing director.
b A partner in a consulting engineering firm.
c The managing director of an architectural firm.

i In various ways; we have a lot of choice.
ii We do what improves the working relationship best.
iii It depends on the circumstances.

Planning hospitality

2 Listen to two people discussing a visit by a group from Saudi Arabia.
This is a short version of the conversation. Indicate who is speaking (**A** or **B**), and fill in the gaps.

[A] We've got .... over from the Riyadh office next week.
[ ] Any ideas on .... ?
[ ] How long are they going to be here for?
[ ] They are arriving .... and leaving at 5 o'clock on Wednesday.
[ ] I imagine they might like to have a look around the town, ... , and possibly some shopping.
[ ] Then .... ?
[ ] That's .... We can arrange a brief sightseeing tour and .... mall.
[ ] But I think .... in the evening.

Adverbs of frequency

3 Put the words in brackets in the most natural position in the sentences.

e.g. We take clients sightseeing. (sometimes)
We sometimes take clients sightseeing.

a Where do you take your foreign clients? (usually) ....
b Do you take them on a river boat trip? (ever) ....
c We take customers to sports events. (almost never) ....
d We don't go to the opera. (often) ....
e They meet at the airport. (nearly always) ....
f We go out if there's time, but we just go to the canteen. (more frequently) ....
g I have travelled by boat. (occasionally) ....
h We take clients to a club. (hardly ever) ....

Practice

was going to; prefer/would rather

4 Write the exchanges as shown in the example.

> **A:** *was going to/hoping to*
> *were thinking of/planning to*
> **B:** *would prefer*
> *would rather*

e.g. **A:** she / buy / a new car
B: her husband / keep the old one
A: She was thinking of buying a new car.
B: Her husband would rather keep the old one.

a **A:** he / tickets / opera ....
B: she / the cinema ....

b **A:** I / invite you / dinner / tonight ....
or / you / come tomorrow? ....

c **A:** you / do anything / tonight? ....
B: no I /go to bed ....

d **A:** we / visit / Australia ....
B: but / daughter / Peru ....

e **A:** you / send / 'thank you' letter? ....
B: no I / phone ....

f **A:** we / walk / town centre ....
B: you /go by car? ....

Giving advice

5 Rate the following advice in order of importance.

Optional [1]
Advisable [2]
Essential [3]

e.g. It's a good idea to arrive a little early. [2]

a When you are introduced, try to remember the person's job title. [ ]
b Whatever you do, don't arrive late. [ ]
c You don't have to tip room service, but you can. [ ]
d Never drink too much. [ ]
e If you can, always take a gift for the hostess. [ ]
f You don't need to wear a suit. [ ]
g But make sure you wear a tie. [ ]
h It's best not to smoke in meetings. [ ]
i You should never put ice in the mineral water. [ ]

UNIT 17

Hotels and restaurants

Some useful phrases

Listen to the recording and repeat

Would you like a drink in the bar before we eat?
That's a good idea.
Where can we leave our coats?
There's a cloakroom in the lobby.

Do you have a reservation?
Yes, I booked a table for eight o'clock.
It's in the name of Tomasov.

Excuse me, we're ready to order.
I'd like the rump steak, please.
And how would you like your steak?
Medium rare   Rare   Well done

I'll have the prawn salad for my starter.
Can I have the salad as a main course?
Is there a vegetarian option?

Let's start.   Cheers everyone!
Good luck with the project!
How's your meal?
It's very good. How's yours?
It's excellent.

Did you speak to John?
Did you talk to him about booking the hotel?
Yes I did. He said it had excellent conference facilities.
He told me to book a room with a sea view.
I also asked the receptionist to suggest a good local restaurant.

So what does the article say?
It says that if you invite someone out for a meal, you should pay the bill.
How much does it say you should tip?

Study notes

Do you have a reservation?
Yes, I booked a table for eight o'clock.
Some phrases for when you want to book a table in a restaurant:
Do you have a table for four people at 7.30?
Do you have anything later?
We'd like a table by the window, if possible?

Excuse me, we're ready to order.
I'd like the rump steak, please.
Is there a vegetarian option?
Some other useful phrases:
What do you recommend?
Excuse me, what is 'pancetta'?
I'll try the salmon.

Cheers everyone!
In English there is no special phrase used before starting a meal.
You can say for example:
Bon appetite.   *Enjoy your meal.*   *Let's start!*

Did you speak to John?
Did you talk to him about booking the hotel?
Refer to Business Grammar Section 17.12 for more on the uses of *speak, talk, say* and *tell*.

He said it had excellent conference facilities.
He told me to book a room with a sea view.
See Business Grammar Section 5 for notes on reported speech.

So what does the article say?
How much does it say you should tip?
Note how we use *say* when referring to the contents of an article.
Also:
What does the article say about splitting the bill?
Some expressions connected with tipping:
Do I need to leave a tip?   *How much shall we leave?*
The service was very good/very poor.

Practice

An evening out

1 Listen, then label the exchanges using the actions in the box.

An evening out in a hotel

Exchange 1	K	Exchange 2	
Exchange 3		Exchange 4	
Exchange 5		Exchange 6	
Exchange 7		Exchange 8	
Exchange 9		Exchange 10	
Exchange 11		Exchange 12	
Exchange 13		Exchange 14	
Exchange 15		Exchange 16	

a Ask about tipping.
b Ask for the bill.
c Ask for your table.
d Ask people to start eating.
e Attract the waiter's attention.
f Check how guests are going to get home.
g Choose from the menu.
h Collect coats and briefcases.
i Say 'good night' and 'thank you'.
j Make a toast.
k Meet in the foyer and suggest a drink in the bar.
l Order a round of drinks at the bar.
m Order your food from the waiter.
n Place your guest(s) at the table.
o Leave coats, etc. with the porter.
p Suggest moving to the restaurant.

Compare the evening with a similar evening in your country/region. What would be different?

Direct vs. indirect speech

2 Rewrite the following as direct speech.

e.g. He mentioned that they had excellent conference facilities.
They have excellent conference facilities.

a She told me to book her a room with a balcony.

....

b The waiter said that the bar would be closed the following day.

....

c We asked the receptionist to prepare our bill.

....

d She asked if we had the name of the French restaurant the doorman recommended.

....

e I told the waiter we wanted a table for four.

....

f He said that he had left his umbrella in the restaurant the night before.

....

g He told me not to wait for him.

....

h She wanted to know how we were going to get home.

....

Practice

say *vs.* tell *and* speak *vs.* talk

3 Fill in the gaps with an appropriate form of *say, tell, speak* or *talk.*

A: What does the article **a** .... ?

B: It **b** .... that the chairman gave an interesting **c** .... at the dinner.

A: How long was the talk? What did he **d** .... about?

B: It **e** .... that he **f** .... for an hour. He **g** .... he wanted to **h** .... some stories about his experiences in Taiwan, where, it **i** .... , he spent three years.

A: I didn't know he worked in Taiwan. Does he **j** .... Chinese?

B: The article doesn't **k** ....

A: He probably does. They **l** .... he's a very good linguist.

Food and drink

4 Put the words in the box under the right headings. Then think of things you can make with them.

e.g. apple pie
asparagus soup
banana milkshake

apple	asparagus	banana	beef	broccoli	cabbage
carrot	chicken	cocoa	cod	coffee	grapefruit
ham	herring	lamb	lager	lemon	lemonade
lobster	melon	mushroom	mutton	orange	pork
potato	prawn	rum	salmon	sausage	sole
strawberry	tea	tomato	trout	tuna	water

meat	seafood	vegetable	fruit	drink
beef	cod	....	....	....
....	....	....	....	....
....	....	....	....	....
....	....	....	....	....
....	....	....	....	....
....	....	....	....	....
....	....	....	....	....
....	....	....	....	....

Things you can make

....
....
....
....
....
....
....
....

Practice

5 Read the article on eating etiquette, using a dictionary as necessary. Then place the following items in the diagram in the position suggested in the text. How does this compare with standard practice in your country/region?

A typical British place setting

a glass ✓

a dinner plate ✓

a side plate

a main course knife

a small knife for butter

a main course fork

a soup spoon

- Cutlery is usually placed in the order it is needed. Start on the outside and work in. Knives should have the sharp edge pointing towards the left. Soup spoons go to the right of the main course knife. For example, the two knives go together with the soup spoon outside of them.
- Salads are usually eaten with a fork alone, which can be laid or brought with the salad plate.
- In Britain, side plates are set level with place settings and on the left. In America, they are set level with the top of the forks.
- Glasses should be placed at the top right-hand corner of the place setting, again working from the outside in.

From *The Evening Post*

UNIT 18

Corporate entertaining

Some useful phrases

Listen to the recording and repeat

What time does it start?
It begins at 10am and lasts for four hours.
Our room is located in the main complex.
We are reasonably close to all the attractions.
We have a superb view of the proceedings.

The package we provide includes a four-course lunch.
a full buffet souvenir programmes
Our experienced team will ensure ...
... that your day runs smoothly.
... that everything goes well.

Can I make a booking?
Yes, of course. When is it for?
I'd like to book the standard package.
Have you thought of having music?
Why don't you have a hot buffet lunch instead of a cold one?
I'm very keen on the idea of a hot buffet.
I'm not sure about having music.

I'll confirm the booking next week.
I'll try and let you know sooner than that, if possible.
I'll let you know earlier than that if I can.
We can arrange things more quickly, if necessary.
Let me know if you need to make any changes.

It's a very close race.
It's a very good game.
They're playing well.
Good shot!

Study notes

What time does it start?
It begins at 10am and lasts for four hours.
Note that we can use the Present Simple tense when referring to timetabled events:
My flight leaves at 5.
The show finishes at 11.

a full buffet
souvenir programmes
Some other requirements at a corporate event:

refreshments	*a good view*	*entertainment*
helpful staff	*comfortable seating*	*good weather!*

... that your day runs smoothly.
... that everything goes well.
See Business Grammar Section 12 for notes on adverbs. We can also use *in a* .... *way* instead of an adverb:
They organised the event very efficiently.
They organised it in a very efficient way.

Have you thought of having ...?
Why don't you have a hot buffet lunch instead of ...?
I'm very keen on ...
I'm not sure about having ...
Some polite ways of making suggestions and some responses.

I'll let you know earlier than that if I can.
We can arrange things more quickly, if necessary.
See Business Grammar Section 12.6 for notes on comparative adverbs. You can qualify these by using *much, far, a lot/little, a bit,* etc.:
We can do it far more quickly.
It needs to be done in a far more organised way.

It's a very good game.
Good shot!
Some useful phrases for when you are watching a sporting event.

Practice

Authentic listening

1 Match the speakers with the places they take visitors. Where do you take visitors?

- **a** A Senegalese technical programme officer ☐
- **b** A Russian civil servant ☐
- **c** A Brazilian advertising executive ☐
- **d** An Austrian financial controller ☐
- **e** A Dutch customer services manager ☐

- **i** a barbecue house
- **ii** an Indonesian restaurant
- **iii** the Bolshoi Theatre
- **iv** a flower market
- **v** the island of Goree
- **vi** the Kirkehof, near Lisse
- **vii** a night club
- **viii** the Concertgebouw Orchestra House

Sports vocabulary

2 Listen and identify the sports that the speakers are talking about. Choose from the sports in the box.

badminton	baseball	boxing
cycling	football	golf
hockey	ice-skating	motor racing
rugby	sailing	shooting
skiing	squash	swimming

- **a** ....
- **b** ....
- **c** ....
- **d** ....

Adverbs

3 Complete the table. Then use items from the table to complete the sentences below.

Adjective	**Adverb**	**Comparative adverb**
automatic	....	....
early	....	....
extreme	....	....
good	....	....
late	....	....
long	....	....
quick	....	....
realistic	....	....
slow	....	....
smooth	....	....

e.g. *Realistically* I need to know this week.

- **a** Could you get back to me .... than that?
- **b** Our team will ensure that your day runs ....
- **c** It started .... than advertised.
- **d** The computer system checks the booking ....
- **e** We can do it .... if you like.
- **f** It doesn't take very .... to do.
- **g** Everything went .... well.
- **h** If you speak .... she will understand you.

Practice

Making suggestions

4 Complete the suggestions.

e.g. The weather is so warm, it seems a pity to go to the theatre.
Why don't ...you go to an open-air concert?...

a We can't take them out for lunch on the 23rd – that's the day of the production meeting.
We could ....

b The booking office has one box left, but I need an OK from my boss and he's away.
I think you ....

c Our Canadian visitors want to do something on Saturday. Any ideas?
I'd recommend ....

d We can't have a sit-down dinner. We haven't got enough room.
Why not .... ?

e I think the plans for the reception are a bit dull, but I don't know what to do.
Have you thought .... ?

f I can't arrange it tomorrow. I'll be in Berlin.
How about .... ?

Booking tickets over the phone

5 Fill in the gaps using words and phrases from the box.

no parking	includes transportation
a group of five	entrance tickets
any tickets left	the standard package
to the main events	every eight minutes
the booking	

A: I'm phoning about the textile exhibition. Do you have **a** .... for tomorrow?

B: Sure, is it just you?

A: No, it's for **b** ....

B: Just **c** .... , or do you want one of the inclusive deals?

A: Er … can you give me some details?

B: The standard package **d** .... to the site, tickets **e** .... and programmes.

A: What about parking?

B: There's **f** .... on the site. You have to use the special bus service from the main square. They leave **g** ....

A: OK, we'll take **h** .... – I'll confirm **i** .... by email.

UNIT 19

Setting up meetings

Some useful phrases

Listen to the recording and repeat

When's the meeting?
It's in the morning on Friday the 23rd.
We're meeting at ten o'clock.
It's taking place at Volta House.
We're holding the meeting in room 406.

We're meeting to talk about the new contract.
And we also need to discuss the sales report.
I'll send you a copy of the agenda.

Are you still OK for the 27th?
Can you still make the meeting?
Could you let me know by the weekend at the latest if there is a problem?

I have some problems with the date you've suggested.
It looks as if Friday is going to be difficult.
It looks like the room isn't available.

I thought I'd better call you.
We'd better postpone the meeting.
We need to set up another meeting.
We'd better meet on Friday instead of Tuesday.
I'm sorry about this.

Would you be able to join us for lunch?
Is Rose going to be able to come too?
I suggest that we all meet at my place at 12.30.
If I don't hear from you, I'll assume that everything is OK.

The seminar has been put off till Thursday.
It's now been scheduled to start at 3.15.
It's been moved to the boardroom.

Study notes

It's taking place at Volta House.
We're holding the meeting in room 406.
A simple alternative would be:
The meeting will be at Volta House in room 406.

I'll send you a copy of the agenda.
Note the use of *will* for making offers/promises:
I'll do it. *I'll arrange everything.* *I'll make sure everyone has a copy.*

It looks as if Friday is going to be difficult.
It looks like the room isn't available.
In less formal language *like* is used instead of *as if* and *as though*.
See Business Grammar Section 17.6.

I thought I'd better call you.
We'd better meet on Friday instead of Tuesday.
should and *ought to* can be used instead of *had better*:
I thought I should call you. *We ought to meet on Friday.*
See Business Grammar Section 17.4 for notes on *had better*.
We can also say:
It would be better to meet on Friday.

We need to set up another meeting.
to set up a meeting = to organise/plan a meeting
set up is a phrasal verb. See Business Grammar Section 13.4 for other phrasal verbs commonly used in everyday business English.

Would you be able to join us for lunch?
Is Rose going to be able to come too?
to be able to is normally used in formal situations. Less formal:
Could you join us for lunch? *Can Rose come too?*

The seminar has been put off till Thursday.
It's been moved to the boardroom.
These are examples of the Present Perfect Passive tense.
See related notes in Business Grammar Section 4.

Practice

Authentic listening

1 Listen, then tick the meetings the speakers refer to.

	Annual General Meeting	Export managers' meetings	Team meetings	Monthly meetings	Working groups	Formal meetings	Meetings with an agenda
A French union representative							
A New Zealand director of a real estate company							
An Irish export manager							

Prepositions

2 Fill in the gaps with a suitable preposition, where necessary.

e.g. The meeting will be *at* 2pm *on* January 23rd.

- **a** It begins .... 3 o'clock sharp.
- **b** That's .... this afternoon!
- **c** It should be over .... 5 o'clock.
- **d** Another meeting is planned .... next week.
- **e** That's .... five days' time.
- **f** It is taking place .... Mato House, ... room 216.
- **g** The meeting has been put off .... next week.
- **h** Are you still OK .... lunch .... next Monday?
- **i** Could you let me know .... the weekend .... the latest?

Rearranging a meeting

3 Complete the message using phrases from the box.

has been put off	looks as if
hear from you	better contact ✓
to be able	it's been moved
as though the room	be able to make
at this end	in time

Delete Reply Reply All Forward Compose Mailboxes Get Mail Junk

Hi Jojo

I thought I'd *better contact* you about next week's meeting. We are having some problems **a** ....

It **b** .... Friday is going to be difficult for Vera. She isn't going **c** .... to get back from Geneva **d** .... Also it looks **e** .... isn't available after all. Provisionally, the meeting **f** .... till the 23rd. And **g** .... to the boardroom. Would you **h** .... it then? If I don't **i** .... I'll assume everything is OK.

Jill

Practice

had better

4 Match each verb (a–i) with an expression (i–ix). Then write examples using *had better* (*not*).

e.g. We'd better book a meeting room.

a	book	**i**	agenda
b	take	**ii**	sales meeting
c	call off	**iii**	apologies
d	meet up	**iv**	notes
e	change	**v**	AGM
f	read through	**vi**	meeting room
g	attend	**vii**	the time
h	send	**viii**	in the hotel lobby
i	put off	**ix**	board meeting

a ....

b ....

c ....

d ....

e ....

f ....

g ....

h ....

i ....

be able to

5 Complete the sentences using the correct form of *to be able to* and a verb from the box.

attend	come	drive	make ✓	work
operate	speak	start	get	

e.g. I wouldn't be able to make the meeting till 11.30.

a We should .... through all the points.

b We won't .... till after lunch.

c Sorry, I .... to the last meeting.

d I enjoy .... when I want.

e It's hard to get a job without ....

f We all have .... the machines.

g She must .... some English.

h Several people .... the meeting.

UNIT 20

Meeting procedures

Some useful phrases

Listen to the recording and repeat

Shall we begin?
There's a lot to get through.
Has everyone got a copy of the agenda?
So, there are four main topics on the agenda.
Let's start with item 1.

Our main aim is to approve the budget increases.
Mark, what's your opinion?
I believe you want to say something about this.

As you know, I'm in favour of the plan.
I'm opposed to spending any more money.
I'm afraid I totally disagree.
I don't agree with what Mark said.

Can we deal with point 3 later?
Can we move on to the next item?
I'd like to summarise what we have agreed.

In the first line, it says smoking will be banned.
In the second paragraph, it only refers to a ban in 'enclosed areas'.

If we don't discuss this now, we'll never discuss it.
If we didn't spend so much on outsourcing, we'd have more money to do the work ourselves.
If I were you, I'd check the facts very carefully.

Shall we vote on the proposal?
Those in favour? Those against?
The motion is carried.
Thank you. I suggest we leave it there.

Study notes

So, there are four main topics on the agenda.
Let's start with item 1.
Some common agenda items/points:
minutes of the previous meeting *apologies for absence*
setting a date for the next meeting *other business*

Mark, what's your opinion?
Note how we often use a person's name to attract his/her attention.

As you know, I'm in favour of the plan.
I'm afraid I totally disagree.
Some useful phrases for expressing agreement and disagreement.
We can also use *for* and *against*: *I'm for it.* *I'm against it.*
See Business Grammar Section 18.5.

Can we deal with point 3 later?
Can we move on to the next item?
Phrases for postponing the discussion and for moving on. Also:
Let's leave that till the next meeting.
We don't really have time to discuss that now.

In the first line, it says smoking will be banned.
In the second paragraph, it only refers to a ban in ...
See Business Grammar Section 17.10 for some useful language for referring to documents.

If we don't discuss this now, we'll never discuss it.
Check the use of the First Conditional in Business Grammar Section 3.1.

If we didn't spend so much on outsourcing, we would ...
If I were you, I'd check the facts very carefully.
For notes on the Conditional in English, see Business Grammar Section 3, specifically 3.2 for notes on the Second Conditional.

Those in favour? Those against? The motion is carried.
These are phrases used for voting in formal meetings. If you do not wish to vote for or against you may chose to abstain. The opposite of *carried* is *defeated*.

Practice

Authentic listening

1 Do the speakers agree with the statement: 'English should be replaced as the main language of business'? Listen and write notes.

- **a** A Russian civil servant ...Disagrees because English is widely used.
- **b** An American administrative assistant ....
- **c** A French union representative ....
- **d** An English production manager ....
- **e** A Scottish accountant ....

Referring to documents

2 Read the article, using a dictionary where necessary. Now listen to the questions, and answer them below.

Meetings might be considered by some executives to be essential for the decision-making process, but they are not always the best place to actually take a decision.

As President of the United States, Dwight Eisenhower used Cabinet meetings to hear opinions. Decisions were made later, in the Oval Office. He never told anyone what he was thinking until the very end of the meeting, hoping that would encourage people to tell him the truth.

Joseph Stalin, on the other hand, showed his cards right away. He told everyone at the beginning exactly where he stood and what he intended to do, then invited comments. Not surprisingly, everyone agreed with him.

If you believe Parkinson's Law, meetings take as much time as you have allotted, regardless of the amount of time that is actually necessary. In others words, a problem worth 30 minutes will become a 60-minute problem if the meeting is scheduled to last an hour.

One way to insure against that is to remove the chairs from the meeting room. Corporate guru Robert Townsend notes: 'No one will believe that you are serious about this. But eventually they get very uncomfortable and can hardly wait to get the meeting over.'

From an article by Jeffrey Robinson

e.g. In the second paragraph, second line, what is the word at the end of the line?
...Cabinet.

- **a** ....
- **b** ....
- **c** ....
- **d** ....
- **e** ....

Practice

Phrases used in meetings

3 Match the phrases (a–n) with the times when they might be used in a meeting (i–iv). Some may be used at more than one time.

i at the beginning of a meeting
ii at the end of an meeting
iii during the discussion of a point
iv at the end of a point/stage

a Has everyone got an agenda? ☐
b Can we move on to the next item? ☐
c I have to say that I'm opposed to it. ☐
d There are two main topics on the agenda. ☐
e I think we can call it a day. ☐
f Shall we vote on the proposal then? ☐
g Can we deal with that point later? ☐
h I think we should begin. ☐
i Joe, I'd like you to outline the current position. ☐
j I suggest we leave it there. ☐
k Those in favour? ☐
l As you know ... ☐
m Can I say something? ☐
n Is there anything anyone wants to add? ☐

Second Conditional

4 Complete the sentences with an appropriate form of the verbs in brackets.

e.g. I *would do* it for you if I *had* time. (do/have)

a If they .... most smokers .... the ban. (not smoke/support)
b .... to make it if we .... the meeting for tomorrow? (you be able/arrange)
c If we .... more, we .... better quality. (pay/get)
d I .... the facts, if I .... you. (check/be)
e The speaker .... it if you .... questions until the end. (prefer/not ask)
f What .... if you .... in my position? (you do/be)
g .... better if we .... after lunch? (it be/start)
h If I .... to go to this meeting, I .... it myself. (not have/do)

Agreements and disagreements

5 Match the statements (a–e) with the responses (i–v).

a I'm afraid I disagree with you completely. iii
b I'm in favour of the plan. ☐
c I'm opposed to spending more. ☐
d We're in agreement on most points. ☐
e I don't agree with that. ☐

i But we can't agree on the price.
ii Why not? It seems OK to me.
iii I'm sorry to hear that.
iv Are you? I thought you'd be against it.
v Don't worry, the board will never agree to it.

UNIT 21

Meeting follow-up

Some useful phrases

Listen to the recording and repeat

How did the meeting go?
Did you manage to get through the agenda?
Did the meeting overrun?

It went very well. We covered a lot of ground.
We didn't manage to discuss all the points.
We agreed to meet again next week.

Who chaired the meeting?
Who took the minutes?
Anita proposed that Vassos should chair the meeting.
Pilar suggested that Simon should take some notes.
Are you going to circulate the minutes?
I'll copy you all in.

What's the position with NAK?
Were you able to contact the contractor?
How are you getting on with the project?

I thought you were going to send me your proposals.
Did you remember to send a copy to the CEO?
To be honest, I'm not sure I did.
I've been so busy, I simply haven't had time.
I'm planning to do it tomorrow.

Lu managed to send the proposal, as agreed.
We've sent you the action points, as promised.
It's all taken care of.

When is the next meeting?
We arranged to meet again on the 11th.

Study notes

How did the meeting go?
Did you manage to get through the agenda?
Some informal language for checking how a meeting went.
On the negative side:
We ran out of time. *We couldn't agree on …* *Nothing was decided.*

It went very well. We covered a lot of ground.
On the positive side:
We made good progress. *It was a very useful meeting.*

Who chaired the meeting?
Who took the minutes?
Notice these phrases:
to chair a meeting
to take the minutes
to circulate the minutes
to 'copy' people in
to give/receive feedback on the meeting

Anita proposed that Vassos should chair the meeting.
Pilar suggested that Simon should take some notes.
Note these verbs:
to *propose, suggest, recommend, request, demand* that …
For more examples of reported speech, see Business Grammar Section 5.
To 'take notes' is less formal than to 'take minutes'.

Did you remember to send a copy to the CEO?
Note how we use *remember* plus the infinitive:
I remembered to post it. *I didn't remember to back up my files.*
For other verbs which are followed by the infinitive, see Business Grammar Section 6.1.

When is the next meeting?
We arranged to meet again on the 11th.
Some other useful expressions for arranging another meeting:
To set a date for a meeting. *To fix a date.* *To change/postpone the date.*

Practice

Authentic listening

1 Listen, then tick the points each speaker thinks is important in response to the question: 'What are the key factors in organising a successful meeting?'

	preparation	clear agenda	sticking to the agenda	specific time limit	restricted numbers	clear objectives	clear lead from the chair	willingness to compromise	willingness to share ideas	good minutes
An American marine pollution engineer										
A French union representative										
A Dutch customer services manager										

Verbs followed by the infinitive

2 Using the verbs in the box, complete the sentences with or without the infinitive 'to'.

be	chair	circulate	cover
get ✓	have	inform	meet
send	type up	visit	

e.g. Did you manage ..*to get*.. through the agenda?

a Did you remember .... a copy to the MD?

b I think you should .... the meeting.

c We agreed .... again tomorrow.

d Are you going .... the agenda?

e Hadn't you better .... everyone about the change of time?

f We didn't manage .... all the points.

g I'm planning .... them next week.

h .... honest, I've been too busy to answer his letter.

i I'd rather .... a formal agenda.

j Were you able .... the minutes?

Direct reported speech

3 Rewrite the sentences as direct speech, using the prompts in brackets.

e.g. Ai-Lin thought that Jonah should speak to security. (good idea)
'It would be a good idea if you spoke to security.'

a Maria proposed that Julio should chair the meeting. (think)

....

b Saskia suggested to the committee that they should circulate the agenda in advance. (Why don't)

....

c Gerhard advised Tod not to reply. (If I were)

....

d Marcela told Jan not to accept less than 50 cents a unit. (Don't)

....

e They advised us not to be late. (not a good idea)

....

Practice

f Elena wants Otto to report back at the next meeting. (Could)

....

g Gregor wondered if we should change our supplier. (think)

....

h Mehdi asked his assistant to take the minutes. (mind)

....

Questions following a meeting

4 Write questions using the jumbled-up phrases in the box. Then match them with the answers.

i	take anyone minutes
ii	meeting overrun
iii	when next meeting
iv	who chair meeting
v	you get manage agenda through
vi	go how meeting
vii	they go minutes circulate
viii	you able contact contractor
ix	at you meeting yesterday's? ✓

a [ix] *Were you at yesterday's meeting?*
Yes, where were you?

b [ ] ....
It went very well.

c [ ] ....
No, we ran out of time.

d [ ] ....
Yes, but only by 10 or 15 minutes.

e [ ] ....
Raj did.

f [ ] ....
Yes, I volunteered.

g [ ] ....
Yes. Everyone will get a copy.

h [ ] ....
In four weeks' time.

i [ ] ....
Yes, I had quite a long talk with him.

An email relating to attachments

5 Read the email, using a dictionary as necessary. Then fill in the gaps using words from the box.

back	comments	document	attached
engineering	regards	technical	through

File Edit View Tools Message Help

Create Mail Send/Recv Addresses Find

To Mr Chandra Patel
cc Miguel Ferrer
From Ellie Sebert
Date: 27/5
Attachment:
Subject NEW LOADING SYSTEM

I have **a** .... the proposals and **b** .... specifications for the new loading system, which I have just received from Seliger **c** ....

Would you please read **d** .... the proposal **e** .... and give me any **f** .... you feel are necessary at the liaison meeting next week.
I need to get **g** .... to Tom Backman by 17th June.

I've also attached a copy of the agenda for the next meeting.

Kind **h** ....

Ellie Sebert
Transport Manager

UNIT 22

Arranging a visit

Some useful phrases

Listen to the recording and repeat

I'm calling on behalf of Irene Braun.
She'll be visiting the States in July.
She'll be staying in Boston for six days.
She'd like to see you while she's there.
She *would* like to visit you during her stay.

When does your flight arrive?
When do you get to Kuala Lumpur?
How long will you be staying in Malaysia?

What's her flight number?
What's your departure time?
What are your flight details?

Will you be coming by taxi?
Yes, we will. Do you know how much it will cost?
No we won't. We're going to hire a car.

Tell the driver to take the Sumner Tunnel.
Take the first exit.
Follow the signs to Allston.
Turn left at the fourth set of lights.

This time next week, I'll be in Baltimore.
I'll see you in a week's time.

We look forward to meeting you.
I hope to meet you while you're here.

Are you leaving for Vancouver on Tuesday?
Yes, I'll try and catch a morning flight.
But I'm going to spend the weekend back in Boston.

Study notes

She'd like to see you while she's there.
She *would* like to visit you during her stay.
Note that in everyday speech the contracted form of would (*'d*) is often used. In the recording, *would* is used in both its contracted and full form.

She'll be visiting the States in July.
She'll be staying in Boston for six days.
Will you be coming by taxi?
Examples of the Future Continuous tense. See Business Grammar Section 2.5.

Tell the driver to take the Sumner Tunnel.
Take the first exit.
Follow the signs to Allston.
Directions are usually given in English by using imperative forms (*do, tell, follow,* etc.). Note the negative form:
Don't turn right.
Other useful expressions when giving directions:
Make sure you take the expressway.
It's best to take a taxi.
Whatever you do, don't turn left ...

This time next week, I'll be in Baltimore.
I'll see you in a week's time.
There are examples of *in* and *for* in expressions of time in Business Grammar Section 17.16.

When does your fight arrive?
Are you leaving for Vancouver on Tuesday?
Yes, I'll try and catch a morning flight.
But I'm going to spend the weekend back in Boston.
Revise these different uses of the future. Refer to the summary of future forms in Business Grammar Section 2.

Practice

Authentic listening

1 Listen to each speaker giving directions in response to the question: 'How do I get to your office?' Then note down the answers.

a A German lawyer.

....

....

....

b An American engineer.

....

....

....

c A Sri Lankan working in Rome.

....

....

....

d A Swedish manager.

....

....

....

Future Continuous tense

2 Read the itinerary, then complete the examples using the Future Continuous tense.

ITINERARY: MR BENITA

June 6 18.20, arr Kuala Lumpur;
Flight AL 308
By car to Hotel Intercontinental
20.30, dinner with local reps

June 7 09.00, meet Linda Thian, KRT Engineering
11.15, visit to Palford Ltd
13.00, lunch at hotel with lawyers
14.45, car pick up at hotel
16.35, dep Sydney, flight AL 216

e.g. – Will Mr Benita be visiting Kuala Lumpur in June?
– Yes, he will.

a – Will he .... the Hilton?
– No, ... Intercontinental.

b – How .... to the hotel?
– By car.

c – What .... at 21.00 on the 6th?
– .... the local reps.

d – .... Palford Ltd?
– Yes, he will, at 11.15 on the 7th.

e – What time .... the hotel for the airport?
– At 14.45.

f – How long .... in Malaysia?
– Only a couple of days.

g – Is he free at 9am on the 7th? ....

during/while/for + *periods of time*

3 Complete the examples.

e.g. I'll be away for three days.

a I hope to meet you while ....

b She will be in the States during ....

c She's going to be there for ....

d She'll visit you while ....

e You can contact her at the Farrington Inn during ....

f You can do some work during ....

g I won't see you for ....

h Will you have time to visit the pyramids while .... ?

Practice

Confirming travel arrangements

4 Read the letter. Then fill in each gap with a suitable preposition.

Dear Ms Corelli

Referring **a** ....to.... our recent correspondence concerning Mr Hertzum's visit **b** .... the end of next month, I would like to give you his final schedule:

23 Nov Arrival **c** .... San Antonio airport.
Flight LF 234 **d** .... 2.30pm.

24 Nov Visit **e** .... Joseph Adekunle Reception at Rumbanda Inc.

25 Nov Return **f** .... San Antonio airport.

As this is Mr Hertzum's first visit **g** .... your country, he would very much appreciate any advice you could give him regarding what to wear, how to behave towards his hosts, etc.

Could you take care **h** .... the hotel bookings, and let me know the names and contact numbers of the hotels so that I can contact Mr Hertzum, if necessary, while he is **i** .... San Antonio?

Thank you **j** .... advance. I look forward **k** .... hearing **l** .... you.

Yours sincerely

Sandra Olbertz

Sandra Olbertz
Secretary **m** .... Mr Hertzum

Cultural advice

5 Imagine you receive a letter asking for cultural advice. How would you reply? Write an example.

Useful phrases

Thank you for …
I was pleased to receive …
I will arrange/send .... as requested.
With regard to your request for …
May I offer the following tips? …
Please contact me if you need further help.

UNIT 23

Abroad on business

Some useful phrases

Listen to the recording and repeat

Do you find it difficult to sleep on long-haul flights?
No I don't. I can get to sleep anywhere at any time!
Do you find it easy to cope with jet lag?
Is it difficult to stay awake?

I'll call you as soon as I arrive in Moscow.
I won't eat until I get to the hotel.
Will you have time to meet later?
Where will you be staying?

I've booked a four-star rather than a five-star hotel. Is that OK?
Would you rather go by train than fly?
I don't mind. Whichever is quickest.
We're meeting in the morning, rather than in the afternoon.

Are there any delays on the motorway?
Yes, there are some road works about 20 kilometres ahead.
There have been some terrible traffic jams.
Thanks for the warning.

Do your hire rates include insurance?
Yes, they include everything except fuel.
So how much do I owe you?
€365 excluding tax.
Can you send the bill to my company?
Sure. Could you sign here, please?

Study notes

Do you find it easy to cope with jet lag?
Is it difficult to stay awake?

Note the examples of *easy/difficult to* + infinitive in the Useful Phrases. The same principle works with other adjectives:
It's hard to work on a plane. *It's important to get plenty of sleep.*
It's not unusual to have problems with accommodation, etc.
Alternatively we can say:
I don't find it easy. *It's difficult for me.*
Note the preposition *with* which follows *cope*. See Business Grammar Section 13.5 for other common verbs and related prepositions.

I'll call you as soon as I arrive in Moscow.
I won't eat until I get to the hotel.

Note the use of the Present Tense after *as soon as, when, while, before,* etc. in sentences like this. See Business Grammar Section 2.5.

I've booked a four-star rather than a five-star hotel.
Would you rather go by train than fly?

rather than can be used instead of *not* when making comparisons.
Would you rather … can be replaced by *Would you prefer to* … .
See also Business Grammar Section 17.9.

There are some road works about 20 kilometres ahead.
There have been some terrible traffic jams.

Travel problems can occur as a result of, for example:

a bad accident *a crash*
a road closure *bad weather conditions*
a diversion *an overturned lorry.*

Do your hire rates include insurance?
Yes, they include everything except fuel.

Some uses of *include/exclude*:
Our rates are fully inclusive. *The rate excludes fuel costs.*
Insurance isn't included.

Practice

Attitudes to foreign travel

1 Match the speakers with the pros and cons they mention in response to the question: 'What do you like about business trips and what do you find difficult?' How would you answer this question?

Pros	
Seeing new places	Speaker 3
You can concentrate 100%	
Tasting strange foods	
Meeting new people	
The pleasure/enjoyment of travel	

Cons	
Long-haul flights	
No back-up/support	
Using another language	
Being by yourself in hotels	
It's tiring/stressful	
Not knowing where things are	

Everyday travel situations

2 Listen to the phrases and match them with the situations listed.

e.g. 1 – What number is it?
– 217; it's a company called Albas Mining.

a Arriving at a hotel ☐
b At the hotel reception ☐
c Checking train times ☐
d In a taxi [1]
e At an airport information desk ☐
f Hiring a car ☐
g At a service station ☐
h Missing luggage ☐

when/while, *etc. in future sentences*

3 Write the verbs in brackets in the correct future form.

e.g. He ...will phone... us as soon as he ...arrives... in Detroit. (phone/arrive)

a Where .... while you .... here? (stay/be)

b I .... a pill as soon as I .... on the plane. (take/be)

c When I .... New York, I .... to bed for an hour or two. (reach/go)

d I .... till I .... to Berlin. (not sleep/get)

e .... John before he .... ? (you see/leave)

f While we .... at the conference, we .... much time. (be/not have)

g As soon as they .... here, I .... you a call. (get/give)

h .... the details with me before you .... the flight? (you check/book)

Adjectives + infinitive

4 Rewrite the sentences using the words in brackets.

e.g. Would you prefer to travel on Friday or at the weekend?
(rather than) Would you prefer to travel on Friday rather than at the weekend?

a I can't sleep on planes.
(find difficult) ....

b Some people can cope with jet lag.
(it easy) ....

c We are meeting in Paris, not Rome.
(rather than) ....

d I usually go by train instead of flying.
(rather than) ....

e I can't see where we are.
(it impossible) ....

f You needn't reserve a seat.
(it not necessary) ....

g Book a four star hotel, not a five star.
(rather than) ....

h We must complete the job as soon as possible.
(it important) ....

Making arrangements

5 Read the emails in which two assistants are trying to set up a meeting between Allen Fanshawe and Henry Koff. Answer the questions, then write a message you might send in connection with making an arrangement. Use these emails as examples.

a What happened during the previous telephone call?
b When does Allen Fanshawe suggest meeting Henry Koff?
c What is Henry Koff's proposal?
d Will Allen Fanshawe need to miss any of the conference to meet Henry Koff?
e Has Esther Andreotti booked flights?
f What is planned for the afternoon of January 27th?

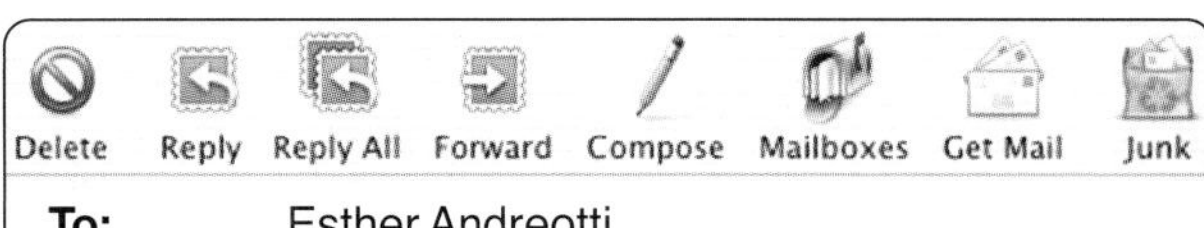

To: Esther Andreotti
SUBJECT: Your telephone conversation with Allen Fanshawe

Hello Esther

Sorry the call was interrupted. If you feel that meeting Henry Koff would be valuable, Allen could possibly return from Denver to New York for the weekend before leaving for Montreal or perhaps even fly to NY for a day from Montreal during the conferences.

Regards
Sonya Craig

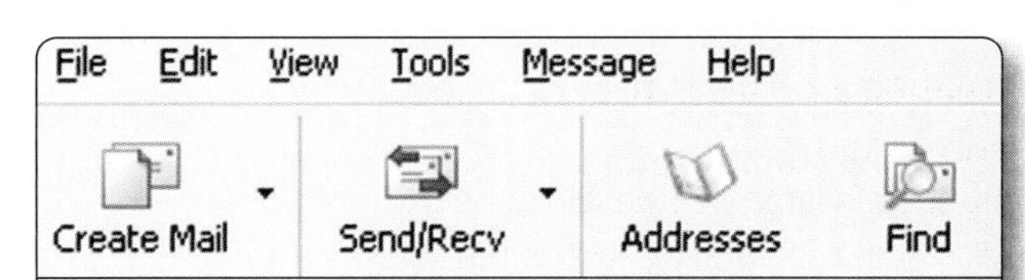

To: Sonya Craig
SUBJECT Allen Fanshawe's programme

Hi Sonya

Regarding Allen Fanshawe's programme, I talked to Mr Koff and his suggestion is that Allen flies from Montreal to NYC evening of Tue Jan 26, has dinner with Mr and Mrs Koff, spends the morning of Wed Jan 27 at the plant and returns to Montreal together with Mr Koff (LV NYC 5.40pm/AR Montreal 6.50pm).

Please confirm if this is OK and I will make the necessary reservations.

This arrangement would leave the afternoon of Jan 27 open, and if Allen has any wishes or suggestions I will gladly arrange something.

Best regards

Esther Andreotti

UNIT 24

Returning from a business trip

Some useful phrases

Listen to the recording and repeat

I'm just back from a trip to Brazil.
I made some good contacts while I was there.
It's a fantastic country!

Brazil is the largest country in Latin America.
It's divided into nine economic areas.
It's one of the 20 richest countries worldwide.
It's a member of ALADI.
What does ALADI stand for?

Minas Gerais is the third most important state in the region.
the second largest   the fourth richest
São Paulo accounts for 55% of the country's output.
It has a population of 33 million.
The main industries are mining and steel production.

How far is it to São Paulo from here?
Not far.   It's a long way.
How long does it take to get there?
Is it a long journey?

What were you doing in Salvador?
I was there on business.
How long were you there?
What was your hotel like?
Excellent. By far the best hotel I have ever stayed in.

I'll send the report today, in case they need it tomorrow.
If it arrives before you go home, I'll let you have a copy.

Study notes

What does ALADI stand for?
Note the question *What does it stand for?* when you want to check the meaning of an acronym or an abbreviation. There is a list of common acronyms and abbreviations in Business Grammar Section 21.6.

Minas Gerais is the third most important state in the region.
the second largest
the fourth richest
See Business Grammar Section 11.3 and 11.6 for notes on superlative adjectives and their uses.

São Paulo accounts for 55% of the country's output.
See Business Grammar Section 21.1 for notes on fractions and percentages.

How far is it to São Paulo?
How long does it take to get there?
Is it a long journey?
These are useful questions when you want to enquire about journeys. Some other possible replies include:
It usually takes three hours.   *It doesn't take long.*
It's a very long/short journey.
It'll take you (up to/more than) two days to get there.

How long were you there? What was your hotel like?
Some other questions for when you want to ask about a trip:
How did it go?   *Did you manage to do everything you planned to do?*
Was it a good trip?

I'll send the report today, in case they need it tomorrow.
If it arrives before you go home, I'll let you have a copy.
Compare the use of *if* and *in case*.
I'll take an umbrella in case it rains. = I'll take an umbrella (it might rain).
I'll take an umbrella if it rains. = I will only take an umbrella if it rains. If I doesn't rain, I won't take one!

Practice

Discussing a business trip

1 Listen to each speaker responding to the question: 'How did your last trip go?' Then make notes about destination, length, purpose and outcome.

Speaker 1: ....

....

....

....

Speaker 2: ....

....

....

....

Speaker 3: ....

....

....

....

Acronyms

2 Listen, then write down the acronyms/ abbreviations and what they stand for.

e.g. EU = European Union

a ....

b ....

c ....

d ....

e ....

in case

3 Complete the text below using *if*, *in case* or *so that*.

Delete Reply Reply All Forward Compose Mailboxes Get Mail Junk

I'm writing my report today **a** .... they need it tomorrow. **b** .... you don't mind, I'll send you a copy **c** .... you can check it before I circulate it. **d** .... I finish it before you go home today, I'll bring a copy to your office, as discussed. But please, only make changes **e** .... they are essential, or the document won't be ready for tomorrow. I agree that it should be short and sweet **f** .... people will read it, but I don't want it to be too short **g** .... it looks incomplete. I'm thinking of listing useful names and addresses in a separate appendix, **h** .... they'll be easier to access. What do you think? Finally, I enclose my email details, **i** .... you haven't got them.

Asking about a trip

4 Write questions using the words given.

e.g. much / cost / get / Preston

How much does it cost to get to Preston?

It depends how you travel.

a far / São Paulo .... ?
It's about 800 kilometres.

b long / take / get there .... ?
By train, about seven hours.

c take / long / plane .... ?
No, under two hours.

d you / do / there .... ?
I was visiting one of our suppliers.

e long / you / there .... ?
I was there for four days.

f your hotel / like .... ?
Not bad – it had three stars.

g exactly / it .... ?
It's just opposite the BMES office.

h BMES / stand for .... ?
Business and Medical English Services.

UNIT 25

Personal finances

Some useful phrases

Listen to the recording and repeat

We spend a lot of money on groceries.
We spend very little on holidays.
We did go abroad for a week last year, but that was unusual.

I'm trying to save up for a holiday.
But I do still spend a lot of money on my hobbies.
About 24% of my income goes in tax.
I pay most of my bills by direct debit.
But I do need to clear my overdraft.

Have you claimed your travel expenses yet?
Not yet. What can you claim for?
The company will pay for dinner.
All travel expenses are reimbursed.

Have you seen the figures?
How much did you spend on eating out last year?
Expenditure was up.
Expenditure was similar to last year.

I normally spend about half as much as she spends on books.
... twice as much as she spends.
... far more than she spends.

Our house was broken into last night.
The thieves took the TV. It's worth about $500.
Are you insured?
Yes, I'll have to make a claim on my insurance (policy).

Study notes

We spend a lot of money on groceries.
We spend very little on holidays.
Note that we spend money *on* things.

We did go abroad for a week last year, but that was unusual.
I do still spend a lot of money on my hobbies.
I do need to clear my overdraft.
do and *did* are used in these sentences for emphasis. Normally we say:
I went abroad last year and I spent quite a lot of money on my hobbies, etc.
See Business Grammar Section 1.8.

About 24% of my income goes in tax.
I pay most of my bills by direct debit.
Some common personal financial expressions:

income tax	*sales tax (VAT)*	*inheritance tax*
by direct debit	*by bank transfer*	*by credit card*
income	*outgoings*	*expenditure*

Check unfamiliar terms in the glossary of business-related terms on page 118.

Have you claimed your travel expenses yet?
All travel expenses are reimbursed.
Expenditure was similar to last year.
These are some other useful financial terms. Check the glossary (page 118) for a fuller selection.

I normally spend about half as much as she spends on books.
Notice how we use fractions in comparisons. Other examples:
I spent double that (amount) on books. *It was three times that (amount).*
It was a third as much (as that).

Are you insured?
Yes, I'll have to make a claim on my insurance (policy).
Note the common insurance terms in Useful Phrases. Some prepositional use:

To claim on a policy. *To insure yourself for/against theft.*
To insure the piano for €2000. *To settle a claim* (no preposition).

Practice

Comparing prices

1 Listen to the speaker comparing prices in Iceland and the UK. First, indicate whether the statements are true [T] or false [F]. Then summarise why the speaker recommends so strongly a trip to Iceland.

a Iceland is more expensive now than it has ever been. ☐

b At the time of the interview, the krona had risen in value against the pound. ☐

c Drinks in Iceland are about double the price they are in the UK. ☐

d Food in Iceland is twice as expensive as in the UK. ☐

Some reasons for recommending a visit to Iceland.

e.g. The food is excellent.

Fractions and multiples

2 Listen to the statements. Then choose from the figures in the box the one nearest to the figure being described.

1,000   2,000   4,000   5,000   6,000   8,000

e.g. 6,000

a .... **c** .... **e** ....
b .... **d** .... **f** ....

Prepositions

3 Complete the sentences with suitable prepositions.

e.g. Her situation is very different ....from.... his.

a Expenditure .... postage this year is very similar .... last year.
b What did she spend .... entertainment?
c It's about twice .... much .... last year.
d About a quarter of my income goes .... tax.
e What's the figure .... depreciation this year?
f I spend a lot of money .... my hobbies.
g We usually pay the electricity bill .... direct debit.
h How much money have you invested .... new machinery?

Credit cards

4 Consider these questions. Then fill in the gaps in the text with the words from the box.

Have you ever lost your credit cards?
Have they ever been stolen?
How do you make sure that you do not lose them?

leave	write down	stolen	check
sign	take care	expires	

Did you know that you can help us to reduce card losses by remembering a few points.

ALWAYS **a** .... your cards immediately on receipt.

ALWAYS keep your cards concealed in a wallet or handbag and **b** .... of your card, particularly when out shopping or in a pub.

NEVER **c** .... them unattended, especially in a car, office or changing room.

ALWAYS **d** .... entries on your statement and contact us if you don't recognise any transactions.

NEVER **e** .... your PIN or tell anyone what it is, except any additional cardholders on your account.

KNOW when your card **f** .... and when you should receive a new one.

IF YOUR CARD IS LOST OR **g** ....
CONTACT US ON ...

From Barclaycard

Practice

Home insurance

5 Put the dialogue in order. Then expand it with phrases such as those in the box.

> I'm sorry to hear that.
> But I thought you had an alarm.
> I know the feeling.
> We were burgled last year.

Person A: Are you insured?
Were they worth a lot?
What's the name of your insurance company?
Did they take much?
What's wrong?

Person B: They were worth about $800.
I can't remember. I'll have to check.
They took a computer and some other items.
Yes, I'm going to make a claim.
My house was broken into yesterday.

A: What's wrong? ....
....
....
....
....
....
....
....
....
....
....
....
....
....
....
....
....

do/did *for emphasis*

6 Complete the exchanges using *do/did* for emphasis. Use the words in brackets to help you, if necessary.

e.g. You didn't send us a fax form.
(posted/myself) We did send you one – I posted it myself.

a The accountant didn't check the figures.
(remember / him / doing) ....
....

b You hardly spend anything on leisure activities, do you?
(hobbies / but not much) ....
....

c I'm sure she doesn't fiddle her expenses.
(seen / her / do) ....
....

d Look, John can't have done this.
(was there) ....
....

e I don't think I know her.
(met / my house) ....
....

f (like/new car) ....
Thanks – I've only just bought it.

UNIT 26

Company finances

Some useful phrases

Listen to the recording and repeat

The company has just announced its results.
The balance sheet for this year is very healthy.
The accounts were approved at the AGM.

What's the value of your fixed assets?
What are your current liabilities?
How much do you owe?
What's the total value of the company?

Net assets are in the region of £40 million.
Gross liabilities are just over £10 million.
The company is valued at between $20 million and $30 million.

A key factor in these results is the quality of our management team.
Our number one aim is to satisfy our customers' needs profitably.

What was your turnover in that period?
What were your total sales?
How much profit did you make?
What was the dividend last year?

Productivity increased by 6.5%.
The quality of our service improved.
Overall revenue increased by 5.7% over the first quarter.
Domestic sales accounted for 33% of our total revenue.

This was achieved by offering excellent value for money.
... better service ... greater choice
Tough targets have been set for the coming year.

Study notes

The balance sheet for this year is very healthy.
What's the value of your fixed assets?
What are your current liabilities?
Some common terms found on balance sheets. Check their meanings in the glossary of business-related terms (page 118).

The accounts were approved at the AGM.
AGM = annual general meeting
Note also EGM (extraordinary general meeting).
There are examples of common business acronyms and abbreviations in Business Grammar Section 21.6.

Net assets are in the region of £40 million.
Gross liabilities are just over £10 million.
These are some more balance sheet terms. Note also:
in the region of = about and just over, just under, about the same
For notes on high numbers, see Business Grammar Section 21.1.

What was your turnover in that period?
What were your total sales?
Overall revenue increased by 5.7% over the first quarter.
turnover = total sales
revenue = income

Domestic sales accounted for 33% of our total revenue.
The opposite of *domestic* or *home sales* = export sales.
Note *the home market* and *the export market*.
See Business Grammar Section 21.1 for notes on how to express percentages in English.

This was achieved by offering excellent value for money.
Tough targets have been set for the coming year.
Refer to the Business Grammar Section 4.1 for notes on Passive tense usage.

Practice

Authentic listening

1 Match each speaker with the statement that best summarises what they are saying.

a A Scottish computer sales executive ☐

b An English manager of a fast food chain ☐

c An English partner of a consulting engineering firm ☐

i A difficult time for the business at the moment, but prospects for next year are good.

ii Last year's profits were excellent, but this year business is difficult.

iii Business is going well, but a lot of work needs to be done in order expand market share.

Financial statements

2 The speakers are reviewing their companies' recent financial performance. Listen, then complete the information.

Speaker 1
Overall performance: good
Comments: ....
Trading profit: ....
% change: ....

Speaker 2
Overall performance: very successful
Comments: ....
Trading profit: ....
% change: ....

Speaker 3
Overall performance: ....
Comments: ....
Trading profit: ....
% change: ....

Active and Passive forms

3 Rewrite the Passive sentences in the Active.

e.g. The budget has already been spent.
We have already spent the budget.

a The accounts were approved at the AGM.
The shareholders ....

....

b Tough targets have been set for the coming year.
The management ....

....

c Turnover is expected to rise again this year.
We expect ....

....

d This was achieved by offering value for money.
We achieved ....

....

e We are owed a lot of money by our customers.
Our customers ....

....

f Profits should always be ploughed back.
We ....

....

g The funds must be transferred soon.
We ....

....

h The company is valued at between 30 and 40 million dollars.
The market ....

....

Practice

Financial terms/headings

4 Match a word from column A with one from column B. Then write sentences using the phrases.

e.g. Interest rates have fallen this year.

A	B
interest	factor
fixed	formula
balance	payments
dividend	revenue
financial	rates
key	report
pricing	targets
total	sheet
productivity	assets

....

....

....

....

....

....

....

....

....

Financial vocabulary

5 Write the opposites of these words. The first letters of the opposites are given.

a creditor d ebtor

b employer e ....

c expenditure r ....

d liabilities a ....

e losses p ....

f net g ....

g borrow l ....

Common abbreviations and acronyms

6 Check that you know what the abbreviations in the box stand for. Then organise them into groups.

NATO	CEO	IT	re	AGM
EU	PA	PTO	NB	Inc
VIP	cc	encl/enc	RPI	PR
ref	pp	PLC	MD	Att/Attn
ASEAN	bal	ALADI	EGM	i.e.

Organisations: NATO

....

....

Job titles: CEO

....

....

Company departments: IT

....

....

Correspondence/documents: re

....

....

Others: AGM

....

....

UNIT 27

Payment issues

Some useful phrases

Listen to the recording and repeat

I'm calling about our invoice of May the 27th.
It's about an unpaid invoice.
Can we pay you by cheque? ... by BACS?
We'd prefer to be paid in cash.

We don't appear to have received payment.
The invoice is still outstanding.
It was due for payment on the 26th.
I'm sorry, but we have no record of your invoice.
Could you give me the details?
What was the invoice number?
What was the invoice for?

It was for 25 training manuals at 25 pesos each.
The invoice value was 5,000 pesos plus tax.

It seems that it was passed for payment on the 10th.
According to our records, it was paid two weeks ago.

We haven't settled the bill as we haven't received the goods.
Apparently, there was a query on the invoice.
That's why we haven't paid it yet.
Didn't you receive my message last week?

When can we expect payment?
Leave it with me. I'll sort it out.
I'll arrange for the bank transfer immediately.
Our next cheque run is on Friday.

We'll take no further action providing we receive payment within 14 days.
I'll assume everything is OK unless I hear from you.

Study notes

I'm calling about our invoice of May 27th.
Can we pay you by cheque? ... by BACS?
We'd prefer to be paid in cash.
These are some useful terms to do with payment. Note also to pay by:

bank transfer	*letter of credit*
banker's draft	*BACS* = Banks Automated Clearing System

The invoice is still outstanding.
It was due for payment on the 26th.
In both of these cases the invoice is overdue and should already have been paid.

It was for 25 training manuals at 25 pesos each.
See Business Grammar Section 10.3 for notes on *each* and *every*.

It seems that it was passed for payment on the 10th.
According to our records, it was paid two weeks ago.
Note the use of *it seems that* and *according to*. See Business Grammar Section 17.1.

We haven't settled the bill as we haven't received the goods.
to settle = to pay; *settle* and *settlement* are often used in relation to payment of invoices and accounts.

Apparently, there was a query on the invoice.
a query = a question about something which is not clear.

Didn't you receive my message last week?
The use of the negative question *didn't you* implies surprise. The message is: I'm surprised if you didn't receive it. I certainly sent it!

We'll take no further action providing we receive payment within 14 days.
I'll assume everything is OK unless I hear from you.
For uses of *unless* and *providing (that)*, see Business Grammar Section 3.4.

Practice

Mathematical terms

1 Listen, and write in the figures and symbols.

- **a** The costs will be between ....
- **b** .... of the population are employed.
- **c** The office is about ....
- **d** The dividend will be ....
- **e** It's ....
- **f** The cost will be ....
- **g** Its capacity is about ....
- **h** The profit is ....
- **i** The units are .... each.
- **j** This is a query about your invoice number ....

unless, provided/providing

2 Rewrite the sentences with *unless* or *provided/providing*.

e.g. If you do not pay in full, we will have to stop supplying you.
Unless you pay in full, we will have to stop supplying you.

- **a** We'll start supplying you again as long as we receive payment within seven days.
  ....
- **b** If you could let us have the order number, we will pay you.
  ....
- **c** If we receive an order reference, we can supply the goods immediately.
  ....
- **d** I am afraid you will have to pay the sales tax if you are not planning to export the goods.
  ....
- **e** You can borrow my pen on condition that you let me have it back.
  ....
- **f** If you send it today, it'll be here in time.
  ....
- **g** If you do not send it today, I won't have time to look at it.
  ....
- **h** If we do not sort out the problem immediately, we will lose the contract.
  ....

apparently, it seems that, *etc*.

3 Rewrite the sentences starting with the words given.

e.g. Apparently they paid it last week.
They appear to have paid it last week.

- **a** There appears to have been a query on this.
  Apparently ....
- **b** It seems to have been passed for payment last week.
  It seems that ....
- **c** It seems that we haven't received it.
  We don't appear ....
- **d** Apparently you have paid twice.
  You seem ....
- **e** Apparently they sent the payment last week.
  It appears ....
- **f** They appear to have paid by cheque.
  Apparently ....
- **g** The invoice details don't appear to tally with our records.
  Apparently ....
- **h** Apparently they didn't get our letter.
  They don't appear ....

Practice

each, every

4 Complete the sentences with *each* or *every*. Sometimes both are possible.

a Our accounts department make payments .... week.

b They cost $30 ....

c They will pay $10,000 with two cheques of $5000 ....

d We check the accounts .... two or three days.

e Our turnover has increased .... year since 2002.

f We have agreed that we will .... pay half.

g We have to please .... customer.

h It would be good if .... bill was paid when it was due.

Chasing slow payers

5 Before you read the advert for a factoring company, consider these questions.

- How do you chase up people who owe you money?
- Do you know any companies which use factoring services?
- What has their experience been?

Read the text, then find words and phrases which have meaning similar to the following.

a bill
b unpaid
c ensure
d grow
e late
f ridiculous

You find a **gap in the market** but **slow payers** hold you back.

Customers who delay payment stifle a company's growth and threaten its very survival. It's a ludicrous situation – it's your money and you need it to expand. If only you could guarantee it would be in your bank tomorrow ... Immediate finance against outstanding invoices, credit protection, and the chasing and collecting of overdue payments would solve the problem at a stroke.

From Lombard NatWest

UNIT 28

Preparing for a presentation

Some useful phrases

Listen to the recording and repeat

I'm calling to check what equipment you need.
Are you planning to use a projector?
Do you mind using an ordinary whiteboard?

Is there a network connection?
I'll need a flipchart.
I'm used to working in all kinds of situations.

Is there anything else you need?
If I think of anything, I'll call you.
I look forward to meeting you next week.

How does the projector work?
How do you adjust it?
I'm afraid the bulb needs changing.
Could you get hold of an extension lead for me? Thank you.

Would you like me to introduce you?
Would you like a glass of water?
We'll begin in five minutes' time, if you're ready.

I'm not very keen on speaking to large audiences.
I can't get used to speaking in public.
I suppose I'll have to get used to it.
I'm used to speaking without notes.
I'm quite good at handling difficult questions.

Good morning everyone.
My name's Neil White and today I'd like to talk about ...

Study notes

Are you planning to use a projector?
Note the following:
digital projector (beamer)
overhead projector (OHP)
slide projector.

Is there a network connection?
I'll need a flipchart.
Other useful phrases for checking if items are available:
Do you have an extension cable?
What is the security code (for) ...?
Are copying facilities available?

How does the projector work?
How do you adjust it?
Some phrases for when you are having problems with equipment:
I think it's broken.
The volume control doesn't work.
The Internet connection is down.

I look forward to meeting you next week.
Note the use of the *-ing* form of the verb after *to look forward to*.

I'm not very keen on speaking to large audiences.
I can't get used to speaking in public.
I'm used to speaking without notes.
These verbs take a preposition + *-ing*. See Business Grammar Section 6.2. For notes on *be/get used to*, see Business Grammar Section 17.3.

Good morning everyone.
My name's Neil White and today I'd like to talk about ...
Some typical phrases for starting a presentation. Others:
I'd like to start by ...
I'm going to tell you about ...

Practice

Presentation checklist

1 The following speakers discuss the preparations which they need to make before giving a presentation. Tick the matters which they mention.

Speaker 1

- ☐ the type/size of room
- ☐ seating arrangements
- ☐ whether the room can be darkened
- ☐ think through the presentation beforehand
- ☐ check technical equipment

Speaker 2

- ☐ the type/size of room
- ☐ seating arrangements
- ☐ whether the room can be darkened
- ☐ run through the presentation beforehand
- ☐ check technical equipment

Preparing for a presentation

2 Put the dialogue in order.

e.g. **A:** We'll begin in five minutes' time if you're ready.

B: Fine.

....

....

....

....

....

....

....

....

....

....

....

....

....

....

Person A

On the side, here.
We'll begin in five minutes' time if you're ready.
Yes, but the lead isn't long enough.
Are you used to doing this?
Good. Is there anything else you need?
Yes, sure. We've got one here somewhere.
How are you feeling? Would you like a glass of water?

Person B

How do you adjust the projector?
I'm getting used to it.
Could you get hold of an extension lead?
Perhaps it should move further from the screen.
No, no. I'm fine, thanks.
Fine.

Practice

Verb + preposition + -ing

3 Complete the sentences with a preposition where necessary.

a I'm not very keen .... speaking in public.

b I can't stand .... losing anything.

c I apologise .... being late.

d Do you mind .... using a whiteboard?

e The batteries need .... changing.

f I look forward .... seeing you next week.

g She's very good .... handling difficult questions.

h I'd like to begin .... discussing current trends.

to be used to *and* to get used to

4 Put the verb in brackets in the correct form.

e.g. We used to ....*use*..... (use) slide projectors a lot.

a We're used to .... (not, have) a canteen on site.

b The company never used to .... (employ) students.

c I'm used to .... (work) abroad.

d We used to .... (have) a training department.

e I'll have to get used to .... (do) it.

f I'm not used to .... (give) long presentations.

g The shareholders always used to .... (get) a report.

h I can't get used to .... (chair) the committee.

Expressing preferences

5 Identify the type of preference expressed by the sentences.

i	strong liking	**iv**	dislike
ii	liking	**v**	strong dislike
iii	neutral		

a I don't mind starting early. ....

b I can't stand using a microphone. ....

c I enjoy answering questions from the audience. ....

d I really hate using a projector. ....

e I'm very keen on exploring how to use new technologies. ....

f I'm happy to use transparencies. ....

g I'm not very happy about the late starting time. ....

h I love using colourful visual aids. ....

UNIT 29

Presenting facts and figures

Some useful phrases

Listen to the recording and repeat

These figures are based on a new survey.
The graph shows unemployment trends.
This line shows the rate of unemployment.
The year is shown here.

As you can see, the overall rate was just under 9%.
At this point on the curve, there is a sharp fall.
The level of unemployment falls sharply here.
... rises gradually ... remains constant

Here the figure goes down dramatically.
And here it rises slightly.
The sales figures haven't changed at all.
The figure for calls per day is about the same.

The figures in the left-hand column represent average sales per branch.
... in the top right-hand corner
... at the bottom of the page

Sales average $517 per square foot.
On average, we make a sale every 3.5 seconds.
We now sell twice as much as we did two years ago.
We now employ half the number of staff.
But only one in three of our staff is prepared to work overtime.

I didn't remember to bring last year's figures.
I don't remember sending them.
I must remember to send them next time!

Study notes

This line shows the rate of unemployment.
At this point on the curve, there is a sharp fall.
Note these phrases for identifying points on a graph.

Here the figure goes down dramatically.
And here it rises slightly.
The sales figures haven't changed at all.
These are some useful phrases for describing falls, rises and constant positions. Some other phrases for no change are:
Sales have remained level.
... have stayed the same. *... have been stable.* *... have levelled off.*

The figures in the left-hand column represent average sales per branch.
Notice the expressions used to describe the position of information on a screen or page:
just below, just above, right next to, to the left of, in the background/foreground, behind, in front of are also useful phrases for pinpointing information.

Sales average $517 per square foot.
On average, we make a sale every 3.5 seconds.
Note the use of *average*. See also Business Grammar Section 17.2.

We now sell twice as much as we did two years ago.
Instead of using the auxiliary verb *did*, we could also repeat the main verb: *We now sell twice as much as we sold ...*

Only one in three of our staff is prepared to work overtime.
one in three/four, etc. is a useful way of describing statistics in general terms.

I didn't remember to bring last year's figures.
I don't remember sending them.
Note the uses of *remember* followed by the infinitive or *-ing* form of the verb and resulting change of meaning. See Business Grammar Section 6.3.

Practice

Referring to a graph

1 Listen, and fill in the information on the graph.

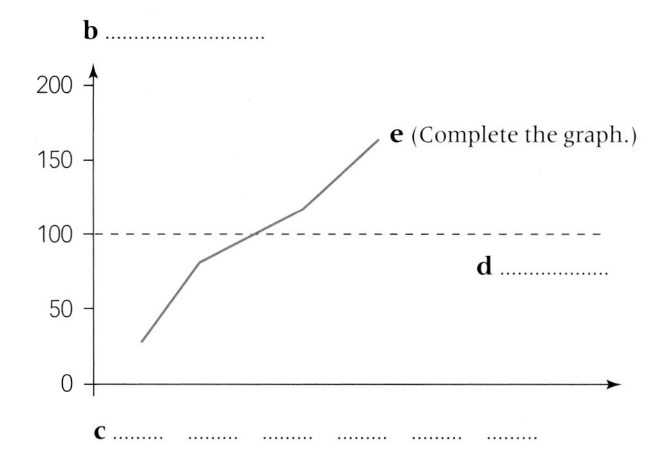

Verb + infinitive or -ing

2 Put the verb in the right form. Sometimes there is more than one possibility.

e.g. Sales started ..*to rise/rising*.. (rise) at the beginning of the year.

a That's an old model. We stopped .... (make) those in 2003.

b I'm sorry. I didn't remember .... (send) you the new figures.

c I don't remember .... (say) that. Are you sure I said it?

d The workers don't like .... (do) overtime, but they have to.

e I watched several members of staff .... (work) without safety equipment.

f One in three workers wants .... (work) overtime.

g I forgot .... (mention) that I can't come to Friday's meeting.

h We can't make them .... (work) if they don't want to.

Prepositions used with numbers

3 Complete the sentences with an appropriate preposition.

e.g. Last year sales improved ....*by*..... 5%.

a This year we expect turnover to grow by .... 2% and 4%.

b .... the year to last August, sales rose by just over 3.5%.

c Unemployment is usually well .... 5% in periods of recession.

d Profits are 10% up .... last year.

e The figures are based .... a survey of 10,000 people.

f The results .... the year ending 31 December were excellent.

Presenting statistics

4 Rewrite the sentences, using the words given.

e.g. Sales fell sharply here.
(sharp fall / here)
....*There was a sharp fall in sales here.*....

a The overall rate was 89.9 per thousand.
(just under / per cent)

b They sell on average £4500 worth of goods every hour.
(sales / average / per)

c Sales average 12 items a minute.
(on average / make a sale / 5 seconds)

d Our sales have risen 100% in four years.
(sell / twice / years ago)

e Our staff numbers have fallen by 50%.
(employ / half / staff)

f Only 33% of our sales are through supermarkets.
(one in three / products / sold)

g These figures show what we sell per city on average.
(figures / represent / our average)

UNIT 30

Delivering a presentation

Some useful phrases

Listen to the recording and repeat

First, I'll give you a brief overview of the plans.
Then I'll say a few words about the takeover.
I'd also like to discuss some current issues.
Our main aim is to increase sales of Fortishka products in Poland.

This table shows projected sales for the coming year.
As you can see from these figures, the projected sales budget is $2 million.
Can everyone see that OK?
Is this better?
Yes, that's much better. Thank you.

With regard to staffing levels, we have 20 full-time staff and ten part-timers.
Moving on to my next point.
That brings me to my next point.
Do you have any questions so far?

As we're running late, I'm afraid I have to stop there.
I'd now like to hand over to Sam.
Sam is going to describe our exciting new product range. Sam …

How did the talk go?
Even though I used a microphone, some people said they couldn't hear very well.
Well, I thought it went really well.
The feedback was excellent.
I really enjoyed it.

Study notes

First, I'll give you a brief overview of the plans.
Then I'll say a few words about the takeover.
I'd also like to discuss …
Some phrases for setting the scene of a presentation and for outlining its structure.

This table shows projected sales for the coming year.
As you can see from these figures, the projected sales budget is $2 million.
Phrases for referring specifically to tables and charts being used in a presentation. Particularly useful are:
As you can see … *As Fariba mentioned …* *This shows …* *Referring to …*

Can everyone see that OK?
Is this better?
Some practical considerations. Others include:
Would you like me to speak up? *Could you turn off the lights?*
Do you mind if I open the window?

That brings me to my next point.
Do you have any questions so far?
I'd now like to hand over to Sam.
Some expressions for managing the stages of the presentation.

As we're running late, I'm afraid I have to stop there.
Note the use of *as* in this sentence. We can also use *because* or *since* instead of *as* in this case.
Note also: *As we are running out of time.*

Even though I used a microphone, some people said they couldn't hear very well.
See Business Grammar Section 16.2 for notes on *even though* and *although*.

How did the talk go?
Notice how we can ask for feedback. Also note:
How was it? *What was the feedback/the audience like?*

Practice

Stages in a presentation

1 Listen and identify the parts of the presentation that you hear.

i	Introducing the presentation.	☐	**iv**	Ending one section, starting the next.	☐
ii	Referring to visuals.	a	**v**	Referring forward.	☐
iii	Giving historical background.	☐	**vi**	Finishing off the presentation.	☐

A talk by a chief executive

2 Read the extract from a talk. Then add the missing passages from the box.

My BIG break

I think my big break was going to Ashridge Management College on a two-week management programme. ... **1** ... Ashridge was a turning point for me. It was a question of the right place at the right time.

It was shortly afterwards that I joined Coley Porter Bell. ... **2** ... Plus, I'm a fighter – not a win-at-all-costs type, but if I believe something is right I'll try to push it forward. So what I've done with the people here over the years is to have very open debates and discussions about where we go, to involve, at key periods, outsiders who've been able to give clear perspectives. ... **3** ... We've always had the determination to find the right answer, which wasn't necessarily my answer.

... **4** ... Over the past ten years we've had boom times and recessionary times, and they've both bought good and bad things. At times I think it was almost too easy to succeed. People lost touch with doing a really good job. **5** I think that's because the business was in reasonably good shape and we worked hard to get it into better shape when times were tough.

Coley Porter Bell is in the business of developing identities. ... **6** ... It is an incredibly powerful focusing point for thinking through who you are and where you want to be going as a company or a band, product or service. Design creates a very simple expression of that, so you've absolutely got to get it right.

From the *Evening Standard*

a I think it's very tough to build a business.

b By this time I had a very clear vision about what I wanted.

c Identity is all about tangible and intangible aspects of a company or product.

d It was while I was there that I fully realised the range of exciting and interesting possibilities within the world of business.

e We gained market share during the recession.

f Outside consultants are good at asking the right sorts of questions.

Practice

because, as, since, so, *etc.*

3 Choose the best word to complete the sentences.

1 .... you can see from these figures, the projected sales budget is two million.
a Since **b** Because **c** As

2 I'll hand over to Carmen .... she'd like to say a few words.
a so **b** because **c** therefore

3 There's not much time for questions .... it is rather late.
a as **b** so **c** therefore

4 It's time for lunch, ... we will have to stop there.
a because **b** since **c** so

5 Our non-Internet business is losing money; .... it is going to be closed down.
a therefore **b** because **c** since

6 Sales figures are down .... the strike.
a because **b** since **c** as

7 .... it's time for coffee, we should stop.
a Therefore **b** Since **c** So

8 Are you familiar with this terminology, ... I can explain it if you are not.
a because **b** so **c** therefore

Phrases used in presentations

4 Number the sentences in the order you might use them.

a Second, concerning our ... ☐
b Finally, how do we see the future ...? ☐
c First, I'd like to give you an overview of ... ☐
d That brings me to the third point. ☐
e Thank you very much. ☐
f That is all I would like to say. If there are no more questions ... ☐
g Good morning everyone. ☐
h I've divided my presentation into three parts. ☐

although, even though, *etc.*

5 Complete each sentence using a word or phrase from the box.

although	because	due to
in case	in spite of	even though

a It went very well, ... the fact that I had forgotten my notes.
b People couldn't hear at the back, ... the acoustics were good.
c I'll be brief, ... I know you are busy.
d I'll leave some time at the end, ... you want to ask questions.
e .... the bad results, we are optimistic about the future.
f .... the bad results, we have had to reduce our sales targets.
g I'll repeat that, ... anyone didn't hear it.
h .... it's time for coffee, I'd like to continue for just a few more minutes.

Business grammar section

1 VERBS

1.1 Present Simple vs. Present Continuous

We use the Present Simple to talk about:

- permanent features and things that happen on a regular basis
  e.g. My brother **is** a lawyer.
  The factory **makes** aircraft components.
  What **does** your company **do**?
  We **don't** often **use** subcontractors.
- timetables and events (see also 2.1)
  e.g. The display **begins** at 10am.

We use the Present Continuous to talk about:

- things that are happening at the moment of speaking
  e.g. – What **are** you **doing**?
  – **I'm** just **typing up** the report.
- situations that are temporary, happening around the present time or developing trends
  e.g. I'**m working** on an interesting project at the moment.
  We'**re trying** to solve the problem.
  How **is** the business **doing**?
  Prices **are going up** all the time.
- personal future plans and arrangements (see also 2.2)
  e.g. **Are** you **going** to the conference next week?

Some verbs are typically used in the continuous, as they can last for a period of time (e.g. *wait, work, learn, study, live, stay, try, rain*).
e.g. It'**s raining**.
I'**m trying** to mend the copier.

The Present Simple is usually used with state verbs:

- verbs of thinking and knowing (*believe, think* (= *believe*), *agree, understand, know, remember, forget, realise, expect,* etc.)
  e.g. – I **think** that's a great idea.
  – I **agree**.
  I **expect** he'll be tired when he arrives.
- verbs of feeling or preference (*want, wish, like, hate, matter, mind,* etc.)
  e.g. The company **wants** to relocate.
  I **don't mind** where we go.
- verbs of perception (*taste, hear, see, smell,* etc.)
  e.g. This coffee **tastes** awful.
  (often these verbs are used with *can,*
  e.g. **Can** you **smell** burning?)
- verbs of possession (*have, have got, own, belong,* etc.)
  e.g. Who **does** this jacket **belong** to?
  They **have** sales offices all over the world.

Some of these verbs can be used in the Present Continuous but with a different meaning.
e.g. We'**re having** some problems with our suppliers at the moment.
What **are** you **thinking** about?
I'**m seeing** Eduardo tomorrow.
I'**m expecting** him to arrive any minute now.

With some verbs we can use either the Present Simple or the Present Continuous with no change of meaning (*feel, hurt, hope,* etc.).
e.g. I **don't feel**/I'**m not feeling** very well.
My leg **is hurting**/**hurts**.
We'**re hoping**/we **hope** to finish on time.

1.2 Past Simple vs. Present Perfect Simple

We use the Past Simple for finished time periods which are specified or known from the context. It is used to talk about:

- actions/events at specific times in the past
  e.g. They **sold** the company last year.
  When **did** you **arrive**?
- states in the past (see also 1.6)
  e.g. I **lived** in Paris for five years.
  (= *Now I live somewhere else.*)
- habits in the past (see also 1.6)
  e.g. I **smoked** 20 a day when I was at university.

We use the Present Perfect Simple when there is a strong connection with the present. It is used to talk about:

- things that have happened up until now in someone's life at an unspecified time (or things that have not happened); *ever, never, before* and *how many times* are common with this usage
  e.g. I'**ve never been** to Australia.
  How many times **have you taken** your driving test?
- things that started in the past and still continue; *since, for* and *how long* are typically used
  e.g. How long **have you been** in your present job?
  I'**ve been** with the company since I left college/for five years.

(note the Past Simple is used <u>after</u> *since* for completed events)

- news and recent events at an unspecified time in the past where there is an impact on the present; the focus is on what has (or hasn't) happened rather than the details of *when, how, why, who,* etc.)
  e.g. The chairperson **has resigned**.
  They **have opened** a new sales office in Madrid.
  Oil prices **have risen** sharply.
  The situation **hasn't changed** at all.
  I've lost my mobile phone.
- time periods which are unfinished (*this morning, this week, this year, this month, today,* etc.)
  e.g. **Have** you seen **Maria** today?
  Sales **have risen** this year.

Note that *yet, already, just, recently, during/in the last/past* are commonly used with the Present Perfect.
e.g. They **haven't sent** the invoice yet.
Profits **have fallen considerably** during/in the last few months.
The company **has** recently **expanded** into the Far East.

In US English the Past Tense can be used to talk about news and recent events.
e.g. **Did** you **talk to** John yet?
I just **saw** the CEO.

Note the change from the Present Perfect to the Past Simple when the focus shifts from announcing news to details.
e.g. **Have** you **heard**? Kai **has broken** his leg.
Really? How **did** he **do** that?
He **had** a skiing accident.

1.3 Present Perfect Continuous vs. Present Perfect Simple

We use the Present Perfect Continuous to talk about an activity that has continued over a period of time leading up to the present. It is used to talk about:

- things which started in the past and are still happening
  e.g. I'**ve been living** in this apartment for five years.
  How long **have** you **been working** here?
- things which have just finished, and might explain a present situation
  e.g. What **have** you been **doing**? (You look exhausted.)

It might not always be obvious whether the activity is finished or not. The context usually makes the meaning clear.
e.g. I've **been trying** to get through all morning.
How long **have** you **been waiting**?

Sometimes the difference between the two tenses is clear.
e.g. We'**ve reorganised** our storage system.
We'**ve been reorganising** our storage system.

In the first sentence, we use the Present Perfect Simple because we are giving news of a completed action. In the second sentence, the focus is on the process. There is no indication that the reorganisation is complete. With verbs involving change, the Present Perfect Continuous focuses on the time period rather than a result.
e.g. Prices **have fallen** considerably.
Prices **have been falling** all year.

We use the Present Perfect Simple when talking about numbers and quantities as there is the idea of completion.
e.g. Sales **have fallen** by 10%.
We'**ve sold** over 10,000 units.

Some verbs can be used with either tense with no significant difference in meaning.
e.g. I'**ve lived** in Bahrain for three years.
I'**ve been living** in Bahrain for three years.

Some verbs are normally only used in the Present Perfect Simple:

- state verbs (*have, be, know, understand, like,* etc.)
  e.g. I'**ve been** here for a week.
  Have you **known** each other long?
- verbs which describe actions that only last for a moment (*find, lose, close, open, close, stop,* etc.)
  e.g. He'**s lost** his wallet.
  Have they **closed** the factory?

1.4 Past Continuous vs. Past Simple

We use the Past Continuous to talk about:

- the background situation at the moment something happened
  e.g. I **was having lunch** when you called yesterday.
  It **was snowing** when we landed at Heathrow.
- what was happening at a particular time in the past
  e.g. What **were** you **doing** this time yesterday?
  This time last year, I **was living** in the States.

The time reference in the past does not always have to be given once it has been established.
e.g. We **were working** very hard to fulfil orders.
The company **was going through** a bad time.

Notice the difference between these two sentences.

We ***were having*** *a meeting when the fire alarm* ***went off****.*
I ***left*** *the building when the fire alarm* ***went off****.*

In the first sentence, the first verb tells us about the background situation (*We were having a meeting*) when something happened (*the fire alarm went off*). In the second sentence, one action (*the fire alarm went off*) is followed by another (*I left the building*). This difference becomes very clear in the question forms.
e.g. What **were** you **doing** when the fire alarm went off?
What **did** you **do** when the fire alarm went off?

1.5 Past Perfect vs. Past Simple

The Past Perfect is used when we need to make it clear that something happened before another situation or action in the past. It is used when telling a story or explaining a situation to establish the background. It is commonly used:

- in *when, by the time, before* sentences (often with *already, just*)
  e.g. When we arrived, the presentation **had** just **started**.
  By the time we got to the airport, the flight **had** already **left**.
  He **had** already **left** before I joined the company.
- with time adverbials such as *the previous year, before*
  e.g. I'**d** never **seen** him before.
  The previous year, the situation **had been** much worse.

- with *because* (to give reasons)
  e.g. The order was delayed because the machine **had broken down**.
- with *said, told, asked,* etc. (see also 5.1)
  e.g. They said they **had sent** the order.
- with verbs like *thought, found, discovered, realised*
  e.g. We discovered (that) there **had been** problems.
  She realised (that) she **had made** a mistake.

Note the difference between these two sentences.

The meeting ***started*** *when the managing director* ***arrived****.*
The meeting ***had*** *(already)* ***started*** *when the managing director* ***arrived****.*

In the first sentence, the meeting started after the MD arrived. In the second, it started before the MD arrived.

1.6 *used to*

used to + the infinitive is used:

- for regular actions in the past that no longer happen
  e.g. I **used to go jogging** every day.
- for past situations that are no longer true
  e.g. He **used to live** in Stockholm.
  We **used to use** an advertising agency.

Note that negatives and questions are formed with *did/didn't* and no *-d*.
e.g. **Didn't** you **use to work** in Sales?
We **didn't use to get** so many complaints.

There used to be is used to describe past situations that no longer exist.
e.g. **There used to be** an old school on that site.
(*There isn't one now.*)
There didn't use to be much demand for that size.
(*There is now.*)
Didn't there use to be a car park here?
(*There isn't one now.*)

1.7 *was/were going/hoping/planning to/thinking of*

These can be used for:

- changed plans
  e.g. **I was going/hoping/planning to go skiing** (*but I hurt my back and had to cancel the trip*).
  I was thinking of buying a bigger house (*but decided I couldn't afford it*).
- tentative suggestions and invitations
  e.g. – **Were** you **planning to do** anything tomorrow night?
  – Not really, no.
  – **I was thinking of going** to see a film.
  – That sounds a good idea.

1.8 *do* and *did* for emphasis

do and *did* can be used in affirmative sentences for emphasis. They are always stressed when spoken.
e.g. I ***do*** **hope** you enjoy your holiday.
The team ***did*** **play** well on Saturday.

Sometimes it is used when there is a difference of opinion.
e.g. We ***do*** clearly **state** that goods can only be exchanged with a receipt.
I ***did*** **confirm** the flight. (*So why isn't there a seat for me?*)

2 TALKING ABOUT THE FUTURE

We can use several tenses to talk about the future. In some situations (e.g. talking about arrangements) more than one tense could be used with little or no change in meaning.

2.1 Present Simple

We use the Present Simple:

- for scheduled events, timetables and arrangements
  e.g. What time **does** the talk **start**?
  We **arrive** in New York at 7am.
- with the verb *be* to talk about how long
  e.g. How long **are** you here for?
  I'**m** here until the 17th.

2.2 Present Continuous

We use the Present Continuous for personal plans and arrangements (a future time reference must either be stated or understood from the context).
e.g. What **are** you **doing** this weekend?
I'**m leaving** on Saturday.
She'**s staying** at the Plaza Hotel.

2.3 *going to*

We use *going to* + infinitive:

- for intentions, plans and decisions that have been made before the moment of speaking
  e.g. What **are** you **going to do** for your holiday this year?
  Today I'**m going to talk about** our new overseas markets.
  I'**m going to look for** another job.
- for predictions based on present evidence
  e.g. The profits **are going to be** very good this year.
  The staff **aren't going to like** the decision.

2.4 *will*

We use *will* + infinitive:

- for sudden decisions made at the moment of speaking (it is often used on the phone)
  e.g. I'**ll call** you **back** in half an hour.
  I'**ll send** you an email with all the details.

- for arranged events (but not personal plans); this usage has quite a formal feel
  e.g. The Prime Minister **will have talks** with the President.
  The meeting **will start** at 11am.
- for confirming things
  e.g. So you'**ll contact** me by the end of the week?
- for promises and threats
  e.g. I'**ll do it** immediately.
  I **won't forget**.
- for predictions (especially with *think, expect*)
  e.g. I expect I'**ll be** a bit late.
  I don't think our sales figures **will be** very good this year.
- for offers
  e.g. I'**ll give** you a lift to the station.

2.5 Future Continuous

We use the Future Continuous (*will* + *be* + *-ing*) for:

- arrangements and schedules
  e.g. I'**ll be staying** for three nights.
  When **will** you **be arriving**?
  I'm afraid Mr Sanchez **won't be coming** to the meeting.

(this use is similar to the use of the Present Continuous but has a less personal feel; it is often used when referring to a schedule or a situation outside the speaker's control)

- for things that will be happening at a specific time in the future (this is the future equivalent of the Past Continuous)
  e.g. This time next week I'**ll be lying** on a beach.
  Do you think you **will** still **be working** here this time next year?

2.6 *when, as soon as, while, before, until* in future sentences

We use the Present Simple (not *will*) after *when, as soon as, while, after, before* and *until* when they refer to the future.
e.g. We'll call you **when** the goods **are** in stock.
I'll ask her to ring you **as soon as** she **gets in**.
Will you have any time for sightseeing **while** you'**re** in London?
Will you be seeing Mr Kim **before** he **leaves**?
Wait **until** I **get** there.

3 CONDITIONALS

3.1 First Conditional

This is used to talk about the probable consequences of possible future actions or situations. The basic form of the First Conditional is:

if + Present Simple (= *if* clause), *will* + infinitive (= main clause).

e.g. If we **don't deliver** this order on time, we **will lose** the contract.
How long **will** it **take** if we **go** by car?

Imperative forms and modal verbs can also be used in the main clause.
e.g. If she **rings**, **tell** her I'll call her later.
If there'**s** time, I **might do** some sightseeing.

Note in conditional sentences, the *if* clause can be the first or second clause. If it is in first position, the *if* clause is followed by a comma.

3.2 Second Conditional

The basic form is: *if* + Past Simple, *would* + infinitive. It is used:

- when the idea expressed in the *if* clause is possible but not thought so likely to happen as in a First Conditional situation
  e.g. If they **offered** me promotion, I **would take** it.
  If I **didn't go** to the meeting, **would** it **be** a big problem?
- when the idea in the *if* clause is contrary to what is known to be true
  e.g. If I **had** my car, I'**d give** you a lift. (*but I* ***haven't*** *got my car*).
  If I **didn't like** my job, I'**d leave** (*but I* ***do*** *like my job*).
- in the phrase *if I were you* to give advice:
  e.g. If I **were** you, I'**d have** a word with the manager.
  (note *were* is frequently used with *I/we* as an alternative to *was*)

3.3 First vs. Second Conditional

When the *if* clause refers to a situation which is possible in the future, the choice of conditional indicates how likely the speaker thinks it is to happen. The choice is therefore determined by the context.
e.g. If interest rates **go up**, we'**ll be** in trouble.
If interest rates **went up**, we'**d be** in trouble.

Note the first sentence indicates that there has probably already been speculation about interest rates going up and that a decision is expected quite soon. The second sentence is much more hypothetical. It might be used in a discussion about whether it would be a good idea to borrow some money.

3.4 *unless, providing, provided, in case*

unless can be used instead of *if ... not* with present and future meaning.
e.g. **Unless** you **call**, we'**ll assume** you'll be arriving around 8.
= *If* you *don't* call ...

Note *if ... not* is preferred in threats and warnings.

e.g. **If** you're **not** careful, you'll break it.
If you **don't** reply within 14 days, we'll take legal action.

providing/provided can be used instead of *if* with present and future meaning when we want to emphasise the condition.
e.g. **Providing** everything **runs** smoothly, we'**ll be able to reach** our target.
Provided the machine **doesn't break down**, the **order will** be ready on time.

in case + Present Simple is used when we take action in advance to avoid a problematic situation in the future.
e.g. We'd better reserve a table **in case** the restaurant **is** busy.

Compare *We'll leave early in case there's a lot of traffic.*
with *We'll turn off the motorway if there's a lot of traffic.*

In the first sentence the action (*leave early*) will take place before the situation in the *in case* clause (*there's a lot of traffic*). In the second sentence the action (*turn off the motorway*) will only take place if the situation happens (i.e. there is a lot of traffic).

4 THE PASSIVE

4.1 Passive forms

The passive is formed with the verb *to be* + past participle.

Affirmative:

The clothes	**are**	**made**	by hand.
The flight	**has been**	**cancelled**.	
The company	**was**	**founded**	in 1909.
The goods	**should be**	**delivered**	tomorrow.

Negative:

The meeting	**is not going to be**	**held**	in this room.
We	**weren't**	**invited**	to the talk.

Questions:

	Has	the invoice	**been**	**sent out**?
When	**will**	the decision	**be**	**announced**?
Why	**was**	the meeting		**postponed**?

The passive is always used for a reason. It is not simply another way of saying the active form. We use the passive in three ways.

- When we do not know or are not interested in the person or thing which performs the action (the agent).
  e.g. The figures **are checked** very carefully. (*We are not interested in who checks them.*)

The Present Simple passive is commonly used in process description to avoid mentioning the agent (usually a machine).
e.g. The chocolates **are wrapped** and **packed** into boxes (*by the machine*).

If the agent is important, *by* + agent is used.
e.g. The factory **will be** officially opened *by the Mayor*.

- To focus on the object of the active sentence by shifting it to the beginning of the passive sentence (subject position).
  e.g. Television **was invented** by John Logie Baird.

The use of the passive allows *television* to be the main theme of the sentence.

- When we want to create a formal, impersonal style.
  e.g. Shoplifters **will be prosecuted**.
  Protective clothing **must be worn**.
  You **will be notified** in due course.

In informal language, to avoid using the passive, we often use the pronouns *you, we, they*.
e.g. **They're bringing in** a new law. (*they* = the government)

4.2 *have/get something done*

have/get + noun + past participle is used when we get someone else to do something for us.
e.g. We only **had** the copier **serviced** two weeks ago.

It is often used after modal verbs.
e.g. We **need to get** the printer **repaired**.
We **must have** the windows **cleaned**.

5 REPORTED SPEECH

5.1 Reported statements

When we report what someone said, we use verbs like *said, told* and *mentioned*. *That* can be left out.
e.g. She **said** (**that**) the hotel was full.
He **mentioned** (**that**) he had been there before.

After *told*, we need to use a noun or pronoun (*me, him*, etc.).
e.g. He **told me** (that) he was going to Australia.

If the reporting verb is in the past, we usually shift the verb in the reported statement back one tense.
e.g. The flight **is** delayed.→
*She said (that) the flight **was** delayed.*
We'**re going to** shut down the factory. →
*They said they **were going to** shut down the factory.*
I'**ve lost** my wallet. →
*He told me he **had lost** his wallet.*
I **hated** school as a child. →
*He said she **had hated** school as a child.*

will changes to *would* and *can* to *could*.
e.g. I'**ll be** back by 11. →
*He said (that) he **would be** back by 11.*
You **can** eat in the staff restaurant. →
*They told us we **could** eat in the staff restaurant.*

The modals *would, should, ought to, could* and *might* do not change. *have (got) to* (and usually *must*) change to *had to*.
e.g. She said she **might** go to the conference.
He told me he **had to** work late.

If the information we report has not happened yet or is always true, we often do not change the tense of the verb.

e.g. **I'm going** to Scotland this summer. →
*He said **he's going** (or **he was going**) to Scotland this summer.*
We **do** shift work. →
*He said they **do** (or **did**) shift work.*

After *suggested* and *proposed* we can use the following structures.

e.g. She **suggested (that) I should talk** to the finance director.
She **suggested (that) I talk** to the finance director.

Note the following changes in time and place references:

yesterday → the day before/the previous day
tomorrow → the next/following day
last year → the previous year/the year before
next year → the next/following year
here → here/there
this → that

e.g. **Last year** was a good year. →
*He said that **the previous year** had been a good year.*

5.2 Reported questions

asked is the most commonly used verb in reported questions. It is often followed by a noun or pronoun. Note that in reported questions we do not use question grammar: *do/did*, etc. are not used and word order is normal subject + verb.

- *wh-* questions
  e.g. When **is the meeting**? →
  *He asked (me) when **the meeting was**.* (not *when was the meeting*)
  Where **do you work**? →
  *She asked (me) where **I worked**.* (not *where do I work*)
- *yes/no* questions
  e.g. **Do you have** any seats available? →
  *He asked me **if/whether we had** any seats available.*
  Is it possible to change? →
  *She asked **if/whether it was** possible to change.*
  Will they take on any more staff? →
  *The finance manager asked **if/whether they would** take on any more staff.*

Note these structures are also used after phrases like: *Do you know ..., Can you tell me ...* and *wondered* (see also section 15.1).

e.g. **Do you know** what time **the next train leaves**?
She **wondered if they would take on** more staff.

5.3 Reported requests and commands

We can also report the meaning of a command, a request, advice, etc. by using: *I/we*, etc., *told/asked/advised*, etc., *me/her*, etc., (*not*) *to ...* .

e.g. I **told her not to park** in that space. (*Don't park ...*)
He asked me to give him a lift. (*Could you ...*)
She **advised me to take** an earlier train. (*You ought to ...*)

Note also how this structure is used with *want*.

e.g. They **wanted us to give** them a discount.

6 INFINITIVE AND *-ING* FORM

6.1 Infinitive

We use infinitives with *to*:

- after many verbs (*agree, arrange, decide, expect, forget, hope, intend, manage, offer, need, plan, prefer, promise, try, want,* etc.)
  e.g. She **agreed to help** me.
  Did you **manage to fix up** an appointment?
  (note how the negative is formed, e.g. **I decided not to go to** the conference)
- after some adjectives (*common, difficult, easy, good, great, important, necessary, quicker* and other comparatives)
  e.g. It's **good to see** you again.
  I found it **difficult to understand** him.
  The keyboard is **easy to operate**.
  Is it **necessary to book**?
  It's **quicker to fly**.
- for written action points following a meeting
  e.g. GL **to contact** VJ.

We use infinitives without *to*:

- after *do/don't* and the modal verbs *can, could, might, might, should, would, must*
  e.g. Why **don't** you **fax** him?
  We **should let** her know.
- after *make* and *let*
  e.g. They **make** us **work** at weekends.
- after *would rather* and *had better*
  e.g. We'**d better inform** everyone.
  I'**d rather not go** out this evening.

6.2 *-ing* form

We use *-ing* forms:

- after some verbs (*avoid, can't stand, dislike, enjoy, involve, mind, practise, spend time,* etc.)
  e.g. I **enjoy playing** golf.
  My job **involves entertaining** customers.
  I **spend** a lot of **time entertaining**.
- with *need* when it has a passive meaning
  e.g. I think it **needs replacing**.
  (= *needs to be replaced*)
- when the verb is followed by a preposition
  e.g. I look forward **to hearing** from you.
  I'm not keen **on giving** presentations.
  She's good **at dealing** with people.

6.3 Verb + infinitive or *-ing*

The infinitive or *-ing* can be used with little change in meaning after verbs such as *hate, like* (+ *-ing*), *love, prefer, begin, start, continue, intend,* etc.

Note *like* + *-ing* means *to enjoy*; *like* + infinitive indicates preferred lifestyle habits.

e.g. I **like travelling**.
I **like to get up** early.

When *like, love, prefer, hate* are used with *would*, we use the infinitive.

e.g. **Would** you **like to go** for a drink?
I'**d hate to be** late.

Some verbs can be followed by either the infinitive or *-ing* with a change of meaning.

e.g. I **tried to switch on** the machine (*but I didn't manage to*).
I **tried switching on** the machine. (*I did it to see if I could solve a problem.*)
I **remembered to post** the letter. (*I didn't forget to do it.*)
I **remember posting** the letter. (*I'm thinking back now.*)
I **stopped smoking** two years ago. (*I don't smoke now.*)
I **stopped to have** a cigarette. (*That's the reason why I stopped.*)

With some verbs of perception (*hear, notice, see, listen, watch, feel,* etc.) either *-ing* or the infinitive without *to* can be used, but there is a slight difference in meaning.

e.g. I **watched him repairing** the machine.
I **watched him repair** the machine.

The first sentence means you watched an activity in progress. The second sentence implies the activity was completed.

7 MODAL VERBS

7.1 Modal forms

can, could, might, may, must, shall, should, ought to, will, would and *needn't* are modal verbs. Modal verbs have more than one meaning in English. They can be used to talk about possibility/probability, to express meanings such as obligation, ability, etc. and to perform functions such as requesting, making suggestions, etc.

Modal verbs have no *-s* in the singular and are followed by the infinitive without *to*.

e.g. They **might sell** the business.

Questions and negatives are formed without *do*.

e.g. **Could** you **repeat** that?
You **shouldn't drive** so fast.

have to/have got to, need to, be able to are main verbs that can also be used to express obligation/necessity and ability.

Past modals are formed by using the modal followed by *have* (*not*) and the past participle.

e.g. She **must have forgotten**.
He **shouldn't have said** anything.
Could you **have left** it in the office?

7.2 Ability

can and *be able to* are used to express ability; *be able to* can be used in various forms (e.g. the past, future, infinitive, *-ing* forms).

e.g. I **wasn't able to get** there in time.
(= *I **couldn't get** there in time.*)
I **won't be able to attend** the next meeting.
(= *I **can't attend** the next meeting.*)
We **should be able to negotiate** a discount.
I **enjoy being able to walk** to work.

7.3 Obligation/necessity

have got to/have to denote necessity or obligation; *have to* can be used in other forms (*will have to/have had to/had to,* etc.).

e.g. We **had to change** our suppliers.

have got to is only used in the present form but it can have future meaning. It is used for specific situations/occasions; *have to* can also be used in this situation.

e.g. I'**ve got to**/I **have to catch** the early flight.
Have we **got to/Do** we **have to reply**?

have to is used to express general or repeated obligation (with frequency adverbs, etc.).

e.g. I often **have to speak** English on the phone.
Do you ever **have to** work at weekends?

need to and *must* can also be used to express necessity/obligation. *must* can only be used in the present form; *need* is followed by *to* and is used with *do/did* in negatives and questions.

e.g. You **must inform** the tax authorities.
We **need to get** a new part.

should and *ought to* can be used to express a weaker necessity/advice.

e.g. You **should check** the contract.
We **ought to get** the machine serviced.

7.4 Negative obligation/prohibition

We use *must not* when something is not allowed or it is very important not to do something.

e.g. You **mustn't park** in that area. It's only for disabled drivers.
I **mustn't forget** to confirm my flight.

7.5 Absence of necessity

don't have to/don't need to/needn't are used when something can be done but is not necessary; *needn't* is less commonly used.

e.g. You **don't have to wear** a suit. It's an informal occasion.
We **don't need to change** trains. It's a direct journey.

didn't need to means that something was not done because it was not necessary.
e.g. We **didn't need to** make a reservation, as the restaurant wasn't busy.

The past modal *needn't have* is used for an action that was performed but was not necessary.
e.g. We **needn't have hurried**. The conference didn't start on time anyway.

7.6 Logical deductions

The past modals *must have, might have, may have, could/can't have* can be used for making logical deductions, i.e. when we try to give possible explanations for unexplained situations. *must have* denotes more certainty than *might/may/could have*.
e.g. – I can't find the office laptop.
– Sarah **must have taken** it. She's working from home tomorrow.

The opposite of *must have* is *can't/couldn't have*. They are used when it is not logically possible that something is true.
e.g. I **can't have left** my mobile phone at home. I used it on the way to work.

7.7 Regret, criticism, unfulfilled expectations

The past modals *should/shouldn't have* and *ought/ought not to have* can be used to express regret or criticism. The opposite of the action/situation expressed in the verb happened in reality.
e.g. I **shouldn't have shouted** at my boss (*but I did*).
They **ought to have sent** a written confirmation (*but they didn't*).

could have can also be used for criticism, meaning something would have been possible but was not done.
e.g. – I'm afraid we'll have to cancel the conference.
– You **could have let us know** sooner (*but you didn't*).

should have is used to talk about something that would be reasonable to expect in normal circumstances but has not happened.
e.g. The order **should have arrived** by now (*but it hasn't*). It was despatched over a week ago.

should can be used with present and future expectations, which can still be fulfilled.
e.g. He **should be back** by 6.

8 ARTICLES

8.1 Pronunciation

We use *a* /ə/ before consonant sounds.
e.g. **a c**ompany
a job

We use *an* /ən/ before a vowel sound and before a silent *h*.
e.g. **an e**ngineer
an office
an hour

When a word begins with *u/eu*, we use *a* when it is pronounced /j/
e.g. **a u**nion
a university
a European

When *u* is pronounced like the *u* in *cup*, we use *an*.
e.g. **an u**nofficial strike

the is usually pronounced /ə/ before consonant sounds and /iː/ before vowel sounds.

8.2 *a* and *an* (the indefinite article)

We use *a* with singular countable nouns. It is used:

- when a noun is mentioned for the first time
  e.g. Could you give him **a** message?
  A man called for you earlier.
  I've had **an** interesting idea.
- when the noun does not refer to a specific object but to any one of the class it belongs to
  e.g. I haven't got **a** laptop.
  Have you got **a** pen?
  I'm going to buy **a** new car.
- when we talk about the job we do
  e.g. I'm **a** secretary.
  She's **a** bookkeeper.
- when we talk about precise and general quantities
  e.g. **a** litre of milk
  a lot of time
- when we talk about speeds, prices, measurements
  e.g. 1000 metres **a** minute (more formal = *per minute*)
  90 pence **a** litre

Note in some languages the word for the first number (1) is the same as the article word. This is not so in English. In English, the usual word for one is *a/an*; *one* is used for emphasis.
e.g. Can I have **a** coffee, please? (not *one coffee*)

8.3 *the* (the definite article)

the can be used with singular and plural countable nouns and uncountable nouns. It is used:

- when we assume the listener/reader knows specifically what the noun refers to; this could either be because it is unique or because of knowledge of the situation
  e.g. Did you give him **the** message?
  I won't be able to attend **the** meeting.
  Don't forget to switch off **the** computer.
  When did you join **the** company?
  The government lost **the** vote.

- when something has previously been mentioned
  e.g. I used to have **a** BMW and **a** Peugeot, but I sold **the** Peugeot.

(note a substitute noun is often used, e.g. ***IM Industries*** *has gone into administration.* ***The company*** *closed all its shops last week.*)

- when the meaning is made specific (by using a relative clause, a prepositional phrase or an adjective, etc.)
  e.g. Have you read **the** report **I gave you yesterday**?
  Could you pass me **the** file **on the top shelf**?
  the travel industry
- with superlatives
  e.g. It's **the biggest** software company in Europe.
- often before the first of two nouns connected by *of*
  e.g. **the** end **of** the month
  the 22nd **of** December
  the price **of** oil
- with some institutions (connected with entertainment, etc.)
  e.g. Let's go to **the** pub.
  I went to **the** cinema last night.
- with names ending in countable nouns (*department, corporation, company, network, authority, union,* etc.)
  e.g. **the** Finance **Department**
  the BBC (British Broadcasting **Corporation**)
  the T-Mobile **network**

(note some names ending in groups are with *the*; some are without *the*, e.g. the Wireless Group, FL Group)

- with some names
  e.g. **the** UK
  the USA
  the ex-Soviet Union
  the Middle East
  the Atlantic
  the Nile
  the Alps
  the Channel Islands
  the Radisson (some hotels)
  the *Times* (newspapers)

8.4 No *a* or *the* (the zero article)

We do not use an article in the following instances.

- With an uncountable noun or plural countable when we are talking about something in general.
  e.g. Industry is suffering.
  They manufacture toys.

Note *the* + singular countable noun can be used in general statements about a class of nouns; *a* + singular countable noun is used when referring to one of a particular class – often before *is*.
e.g. **The** mobile phone has revolutionised our lives.
A mobile phone is essential for business people these days.

Note just the countable plural could be used in both these sentences (*mobile phones …*).

- Generally with names (of people, companies, places, days, etc.).

e.g. IBM	Daewoo
Nokia	BA
McDonald's	Heathrow Airport
Christmas Day	I work in Accounts.

- With some frequently used nouns when they follow prepositions (*home, work, school, university, bed,* etc.)

e.g. at home	at work
at school	at university
go home	go to bed

- With names of meals.
  e.g. have breakfast/lunch/dinner
- With possessive nouns.
  e.g. today's news
  Brown's Hotel
  Britain's economy

9 NOUNS

9.1 Countable and uncountable nouns

Countable nouns are the names of things that you can count. We can use *a/an* with countable nouns. Countable nouns have plurals.
e.g. a **job**
two **machines**
several **languages**
a thousand **dollars**

Uncountable nouns are the names of things you can't count. They may represent mass nouns (such as *oil*), abstract ideas (*leadership*) or general words (*food*, etc.). We can't use *a/an* with uncountable nouns and there is no plural form.

e.g. water	electricity
money	luggage
work	

the, some, any, a lot of, a bit of can be used with both countable and uncountable nouns (see also 10.1 and 10.2).

advice, equipment, information are uncountable. We do not use them with *a/an*, and they have no plurals.

e.g. I'd like to give you **some advice**. (not *an advice*)
Could you give me **some information**? (not *an information* or *informations*)
I bought **some** new **equipment**. (not *a new equipment*)

English (and the names of other languages) are also uncountable.

e.g. She speaks very good **English**. (not *a very good English*)

If we want to quantify an uncountable noun we can use a countable noun before it.

e.g. We need to buy **a** new **piece/bit of** equipment.
Can we have **two bottles** of water?

Some nouns have both countable and uncountable forms, but they have different meanings (sometimes only slightly different).

e.g. I haven't got **time**. (uncountable = *I'm busy*)
Have **a** great **time**. (countable = *experience*)
The printer needs (**some**) **paper**. (uncountable = *sheets of paper*)
Could you buy me **a paper**? (countable = *a newspaper*)
I love **wine**. (uncountable = *wine in general*)
They sell **some** excellent French **wines**. (countable = *varieties of wine*)

Note some nouns which tend to be uncountable in general usage are often used as countable nouns in a more technical sense (often when talking about different types).

e.g. new energy **technologies**
We produce **plastics**.

Sometimes the countable noun and its uncountable equivalent are completely different words.

e.g. I've got to collect my **suitcases/bags**. (countable)
I've got to collect my **luggage**. (uncountable)
The island has a wonderful **climate**. (countable)
The island has wonderful **weather**. (uncountable)

9.2 Compound nouns

When there is a relationship between two nouns we often use a compound noun. The first noun functions as an adjective describing the second noun. The first noun is nearly always in the singular.

Some compound nouns are written as one word.

e.g. the **boardroom**
a **shareholder**
the **workforce**

Some compound nouns can be hyphenated.

e.g. **decision-making**
the **flight-deck**
team-building

Most compound nouns are written as two words.

e.g. a **bank account**
a **computer system**
an **Internet provider**

There are often alternative ways of writing compound nouns.

e.g. **buyout** — **buy-out**
answerphone — **answer phone**
voice-mail — **voicemail**

Note also *taxpayer*, but *tax year*; *shareholder*, but *share price*.

Sometimes three or more nouns may be used together.

e.g. a **management training scheme**
the **company smoking policy**
a **consumer protection organisation**

9.3 -*'s* and *of*

We usually use -*s* (singular -*'s*, plural -*s'*) when the first noun is human. Often the relationship is one of possession.

e.g. **Graham's** desk is over there. (not *the desk of Graham*)
The **directors'** salaries are very high.

Words ending in -*s* usually add -*'s* (pronounced /iz/).

e.g. That's **James's** car.
My **boss's** office is opposite.

We can use -*'s* for nouns that have a close association with people:

- for companies, organisations and institutions
  e.g. **IBM's** strategy
  the **organisation's** headquarters
  the **government's** decision
- for place nouns
  e.g. **Britain's** roads
  New York's Mayor
  the **world's** longest river
- for time nouns
  e.g. last **year's** figures
  today's newspaper

We usually use *of* for things. The relationship between the two nouns is more abstract than the -*'s* relationship and is not usually one of possession.

e.g. the end **of** the **week**
the cost **of living**
the date **of** the **meeting**
the launch **of** a **product**
the development **of** the **system**
the lid **of** the printer

Nouns related to organisations and places can also be expressed with *of*.

e.g. the head **of Coca-Cola**
the editor **of** the ***Times***
the takeover **of** the **company**

the owner **of** the **shop**
the President **of** the **USA**

10 QUANTIFIERS

10.1 *some, any, no*

We usually use *some* in affirmative sentences, and *any/no* in negative sentences. *some* and *any* can be used with countable plural and uncountable nouns. Both *some* and *any* can be used without a noun.

	Affirmative	Negative
e.g.	We need **some** samples.	They have**n't** got **any** brochures.
	We need **some** stationery.	They have**n't** got **any** information.
	You could order **some**.	We do**n't** need **any**.

In *yes/no* questions, *any* indicates we are not sure if the answer is going to be yes; *some* is used when we are more confident of a positive answer.

e.g. Have you got **some** paper? (*There is usually a supply in the office.*)
Is there **any** paper in the printer? (*Maybe that's why it isn't working.*)
Have you got **some/any**?

We normally use *some* in requests.
e.g. Can I have **some** time off next week?

With offers both can be used.
e.g. Would you like **some/any** coffee?

some is also used in *wh-* questions,
e.g. Where can I get **some** toner?

no can be used for *not ... any* when we want to emphasise something does not exist.
e.g. I have **no** news about it. (= *I haven't got any news.*)
There are **no** car parking spaces left. (= *There aren't any car parking spaces.*)

no is also used at the beginning of sentences (*not ... any* is not possible in this position).
e.g. **No** information was available (not *Not any information* ...)

10.2 *much, many, a lot (of), (a) few, several, (a) little*

With uncountables	With plurals
a lot of/lots of/much	a lot of/lots of/many
quite a bit of	several/quite a few/quite a lot of
a little	a few
not (very) much/not a lot of	not (very) many/not a lot of
(very) little	(very) few

Note the following.

- *several* is used with countable plural nouns. It is not used in negatives. It means more than *some* but less than *a lot of.*
  e.g. We have **several** good contacts there.
  Several customers have complained.
- *a lot of* is a little less formal than *much/many; lots of* is even more informal. *a lot of* can be used in affirmatives, negatives and questions, and with countable plurals and uncountable nouns.
  e.g. We had **a lot of** time there.
  Did you see **a lot of** clients?
  We do**n't** do **a lot of** business there.
- When there is no following noun we use *a lot* with no *of.*
  e.g. We sell **a lot** in Turkey.
- *much* is usually only used in negatives and questions, and with uncountable nouns.
  e.g. Did you have **much** time for sightseeing?
  I have**n't** got **much** cash on me.
- *many* is used in negatives and questions with countable plurals. It can be used in affirmatives but usually just in initial position and is quite formal.
  e.g. **Many factories** are closing down.
- *a few* has a similar meaning to *some.*
  e.g. She talked to **a few** clients. (= *some clients*)

However, *quite a few/quite a bit of* is similar in meaning to *quite a lot of.*
e.g. He made **quite a few** phone calls. (= *quite a lot of phone calls*)
We've spent **quite a bit of** money. (= *quite a lot of money*)
Note we cannot use *quite* with *much/many.*

10.3 *each* and *every*

each is used with a singular countable noun when we want to refer individually to one of a group of at least two.
e.g. **Each** copy costs 75p.

It can be used without a following noun.
e.g. They cost £10 **each**.

every is used with a singular countable noun when we want to refer individually to all the members of a group of at least three.
e.g. **Every** invoice is checked before it leaves the office.

We could also use *all* + plural noun to refer to all the members of a group.
e.g. **All invoices** are checked before they leave the office.

11.1 The order of adjectives

Adjectives are used before nouns and after *to be*. The following table may be helpful but the order of adjectives is not rigidly fixed. Generally, opinion adjectives are furthest away from the noun and factual characteristics closer.

opinion	size	age	colour	origin	composition	modifying noun	main noun
a lovely	large	new	white	Italian	leather		sofa
an ugly	old	grey		metal		filing	cabinet

It is unusual to use more than three or four adjectives to describe a noun.

We can use *each* or *every* with *day, week, month*, etc., but with a number we use *every*.

e.g. **each/every** month
each/every Friday
every two weeks

11.2 Opposite forms of adjectives

un- is the most common negative prefix.

e.g. profitable / **un**profitable
attractive / **un**attractive

in- is another common prefix. It becomes *im-* before *m* or *p*; *ir-* before *r*; and *il-* before *l*.

e.g. direct / **in**direct
mature / **im**mature
polite / **im**polite
relevant / **ir**relevant
legal / **il**legal

dis- is another negative prefix.

e.g. honest / **dis**honest

-less is a negative suffix.

e.g. tasty or tasteful / taste**less**
colourful / colour**less**

Note *well-paid* / *badly* or *poorly paid*.

11.3 Comparative and superlative adjectives

Short adjectives (one syllable)

	Adjective	Comparative	Superlative
most one-syllable adjectives	short few	shorter fewer	the shortest the fewest
adjectives ending in *-e*	large	larger	the largest
adjectives ending in one short vowel + one consonant	big	bigger	the biggest
adjectives ending in *-y*	dry	drier	the driest
irregular	good bad far much/many little	better worse further/farther more less	best worst furthest/farthest the most the least

Longer adjectives (two or more syllables)

	Adjective	Comparative	Superlative
two-syllable adjectives ending in *-y, -le, -ow*	busy simple narrow	busier simpler narrower	the busiest the simplest the narrowest
Other two-syllable adjectives	careful modern	more careful more modern	the most careful the most modern
three and four-syllable and adjectives	expensive competitive	more expensive more competitive	the most expensive the most competitive

11.4 Making comparisons

We can compare two things using the comparative adjective + *than*.

e.g. My last job was **more interesting than** my present job.
I'm **busier** now **than** I used to be.

Note also the use of *not as ... as*.

e.g. My present job is**n't as interesting as** my last job.
I'm **not as busy** now **as** I was last month.

not as ... as is often preferred to *less* + adjective.

e.g. My present job **is less interesting** than (*is not as interesting as*) my last job.
I'm **less busy** now than (*not as busy now as*) I was last month.

Note we do not normally use *less* with short adjectives (not *less big*).

To say that things are the same in a certain way, we can use *as ... as*.

e.g. We're **as big as** our main competitor.

more and *less* can be used with nouns and verbs.

e.g. We sell **more components** abroad than to domestic companies.
It **costs more** to produce small quantities.
It **costs less** to produce in bulk.

11.5 Degrees of comparison

To strengthen the meaning of comparatives we can use *much/far/a lot*; to lessen the meaning we can use *a little/a bit/slightly*.

e.g. Their budget is **much larger than** ours.
It's **far more profitable than** it was.
We sold **slightly more** this year **than** last year.

Note the use of *the same as, different from* and *similar to*, and ways of modifying their meaning.

e.g. Our situation is **very/completely different from/to** yours.
My job is **very similar to** yours.
Our position is **exactly the same as** it was before.

We can also use fractions and multiples in comparisons.

e.g. She earns **half as much as** he does.
They spend **twice as much** on raw materials **as** we do.
They employ **twice as many** people **as** we do.
The advertising budget is **three times as much** as ours.

11.6 Using superlatives

Note how we use superlatives.

e.g. This is **our most expensive** range of products.
We are **the best** in the business.
Size is **the least important** factor in this market.

We do not usually use *the least* with short adjectives. Instead, we choose the opposite adjective and add *-est*.

e.g. Our **biggest** market is Asia; our **smallest** market is the UK. (not *least big*)

Superlatives are used with ordinal numbers to talk about rankings.

e.g. It's **the second largest** pharmaceutical company in Europe.
It's the **fourth most expensive** city in the world.

12 ADVERBS

12.1 Adjectives and adverbs

We use adjectives before nouns and after *be*. We use adverbs to give more information about verbs, adjectives and other adverbs.

e.g. They are an **efficient** company. (adjective + noun)
The company is **efficient**. (*be* + adjective)
They work **efficiently**. (verb + adverb)
They work **extremely efficiently**. (verb + adverb + adverb)
They are **extremely efficient**.
(*be* + adverb + adjective)

12.2 The form and spelling of adverbs

	Adjective	Adverb
Most adjectives add *-ly*	quick careful	quickly carefully
Adjectives ending in *-ble*	possible profitable	possibly profitably
Adjectives ending in *-ic*	automatic logical	automatically logically
Adjectives ending in *-y*	easy temporary	easily temporarily
Irregular adverbs	good hard early late fast long	well hard early late fast long

12.3 The position of adverbs

At the beginning of the sentence:

- when the adverb applies to the whole sentence
  e.g. **Realistically**, I don't think we'll win the contract.
- with time adverbs (although final position is more common)
  e.g. **Last year** we sold far more.

In the middle of the sentence:

– before a main verb (with frequency, intensifying and probability adverbs)
  e.g. I **never/often see** him at work. (frequency)
  I **completely disagree**. (intensifying)
  He'll **probably/definitely get promoted**. (probability)

Note these adverbs go after *be* (when there is no auxiliary verb).
e.g. She'**s probably** on her way.
It **was never** reliable.

– before an adjective or another adverb (see also 12.4)
  e.g. I thought the presentation was **extremely good**.
  I thought she spoke **really well**.

At the end of a sentence:

– adverbs that say more about the verb (manner adverbs)
  e.g. We ensure that everything runs **smoothly**.
  I thought he chaired the meeting **very** competently.
  He arrived very **late**.

– specific frequency adverbs and *not ... very often*
  e.g. We have a meeting **once a week**.
  I don't see him **very often**.

Note that adverbs in English don't go between the verb and the object.
e.g. He speaks French **well**. (not *He speaks well French.*)
I always read reports **carefully**. (not ... *read carefully reports*)

12.4 Adverbs modifying adjectives and adverbs

Adverbs can be used to modify adjectives/adverbs:

– to intensify the meaning (*completely, totally, quite, absolutely, extremely, very, really,* etc.)
  e.g. **really expensive**
  completely reliable

– to tone down the meaning (*fairly, quite, reasonably*, etc.)
  e.g. **fairly frequently**
  quite cheap

Note *absolutely* is used with strong adjectives.
e.g. **absolutely awful** (not *absolutely bad*)

quite can be an intensifier or a downtoner.
e.g. I was **quite shocked**. (intensifier)
It's **quite cold** in here. (downtoner)

Adverbs can also be used to modify past-participles.
e.g. It's **beautifully designed**.
It's a very **well-made product**.
That hotel has been **highly recommended**.

12.5 Adverbs of frequency

To ask about frequency we normally use *how often* and *ever*.
e.g. **How often** do you have to travel on business?
Do you **ever** have to go abroad?

From most to least frequent:

always *usually* *often* *sometimes*
occasionally *not often* *very rarely* *never*

To be more specific we can use phrases like:
once a week *every two weeks* *four times a year*

Note that the more specific time adverbs go at the end of the sentence, whereas frequency adverbs normally go before the main verb (see 12.3).
e.g. He **occasionally walks** to work.
I **don't usually eat** in the staff restaurant.
We have the photocopier serviced **twice a year**.

12.6 Comparative and superlative adverbs

	Adverb	Comparative
Short adverbs	hard soon early	harder sooner earlier
Longer adverbs	frequently carefully	more frequently more carefully
Irregular	well badly early	better worse earlier

e.g. I'm sorry I haven't replied **sooner**.
You must check it **more carefully** in future.

Note we can modify comparatives in the same way as we modify adjectives.
e.g. I have to work **much harder** now than I used to.

13 PREPOSITIONS

13.1 Talking about time

in is used with:

parts of the day	**in** the morning
months	**in** December
years	**in** 2000
parts of the year	**in** the second quarter
centuries	**in** the 20th century
how soon something will happen	**in** half an hour (not *after half an hour*)

Note *in the morning* can mean either *every morning* or *tomorrow morning*.
e.g. I usually answer my emails **in the morning**. (= *every morning*) I'll ring you **in the morning**. (= *tomorrow morning*)

at is used with:

precise times	**at** 11am
night	**at** night
lunchtime	**at** lunchtime

holidays and religious festivals	**at** Christmas
weekend	**at** the weekend (US also **on** the weekend)

on is used with:

days	**on** Tuesday
dates	**on** 22 May
special days	**on** Independence Day
days + morning/ afternoon, etc.	**on** Monday morning

See also 17.16 for *during, in, for* and *since*.

within and *by* are used for deadlines.

e.g. We will respond **within** ten working days.
We require payment **by** the end of the month.

No preposition is used with:

- *today, tomorrow, yesterday, tonight*
  e.g. I'll see you **tomorrow**.
- *next, this and last*
  e.g. I saw him **last** week.
  I'm flying to the States **this** Saturday.

Other past and future time references:

the day before yesterday — *two weeks ago*
the week before last — *a week last Friday*
the month after next — *a week on Monday*
in two weeks' time/in a fortnight

13.2 Talking about place

To talk about geographical location

e.g. It's (**to the**) **south** of London.
It's **in the north** of the country.
It's **500 kilometres north-west of** Beijing.
It's **just outside** Frankfurt.
It's **on** the coast/inland.
It's **just off** the motorway.
It's **on** a main road.
It's **in** the centre/middle of the city.
It's **in** an industrial zone/**on** an industrial estate.
It's **in** the suburbs.
It's **near/not far from/close to** the centre.
It's **surrounded by** hills.
It's **beyond** the car park.
It's **on the other side of** that building.

To talk about location inside a building

e.g. It's **to the left/right of** the lift.
It's **on** the ground floor.
It's **at the top/bottom of** the stairs.
It's **at the end of** the corridor.
It's **across** the corridor.
It's **the second door on the left/right**.

To talk about where people are

e.g. She's **at** work.
... **at** home. ... **at/in** the office.
... **at** lunch. ... **at** the airport.
... **at** a conference. ... **in** a meeting.
... **in** Manchester. ... **in** France.
... **on** holiday. ... **on** sick leave.
He's staying **at** the Intercontinental.

To talk about directions

e.g. Go **to** the end of the corridor.
... **up/down** those stairs. ... **along** the road.
... **past** the airport. ... **onto** the motorway.
... **out of** the building. ... **into** the car park.
... **up/down to** the next floor.
Follow the signs **to** Basel.
Take the second exit **on** the left.
Turn left **at** the traffic lights.
It's the third turning **on** the right.

To locate information on a page

e.g. **In** the top/bottom left-/right-hand corner.
At the top/bottom of the page.
Half-way **up/down** the page.
On the left-/right-hand side.
In the left-/right-hand column.
In the third row down.
In the second row from the top.

13.3 Other use of prepositions

She works **in** Finance.
It comes **in** several sizes.
How much are we **in** credit?
There isn't much profit **in** it.
I'm afraid it isn't **in** stock.
I'm working **on** a new project.
Have you got an update **on** those figures?
Our meetings never start **on** time.
It's the third item **on** the agenda.
I work **for** a large multi-national.
The cheque is **for** £500.
There isn't much demand **for** that product.
It's free **of** charge.
They have a turnover **of** £200 million.
We're going out **to/for** dinner.
According **to** your letter ...
They usually pay **by** direct debit.
Sales have increased **by** 10%.

Note the verbs *phone/call/ring, discuss* and *tell* are not followed directly by a preposition.

e.g. Have you **called/phoned/rung** your office yet?
We need to **discuss** this.
Have you **told** her?

13.4 Some phrasal verbs

The meeting has been **put off** till next Tuesday.
We need to **set up** a meeting with them.
I'm **tied up** at the moment.
Have you **made up** your mind yet?
I can't **get through** to him.
I'll **get back** to you straightaway.
We didn't **get through** all the items on the agenda.
How are you **getting on with** the project?
We **ran out** of time.
We need to **sort out** this problem.
I'll **hand over** to Max now.

13.5 Verbs and related prepositions

apologise	**for**	complain	**about**
be based	**on**	cope	**with**
be divided	**into**	deal	**with**
be fond	**of**	do something	**about**
be good	**at**	have a degree	**in**
be/have a record	**of**	have/take time	**off**
be/have time	**for**	have trouble	**with**
be/have something wrong	**with**	hear	**of/about**
be in charge	**of**	liaise	**with**
be interested	**in**	look forward	**to**
be in favour	**of**	make a decision	**on**
be keen	**on**	make a point	**about**
be made	**of**	make notes	**on**
be opposed	**to**	say something	**about**
be pleased	**with/ about**	specialise	**in**
be responsible	**for**	spend time/ money	**on**
be sorry	**about**	tell someone	**about**
be sure	**about**	thank someone	**for**
be thinking	**of**	think	**of/ about**
be worried	**about**	vote	**on**
belong	**to**		

14 RELATIVE CLAUSES

For people we use *who* and *that*.

e.g. **The person who** usually deals with complaints is away.
The applicant that got the job was not the most experienced.

For things we use *that* or *which*.

e.g. I work for a **company that** makes computers.
There are some **jobs which** need to be done immediately.

We can leave out *who/that/which* if it is not the subject of the relative clause.

e.g. **The supplier** (**that/who**) we usually deal with is very reliable. (*We deal with* ***the supplier***.)
Have you read **the email** (**that/which**) I sent you? (*I sent you* ***the email***.)

Note we usually put the preposition at the end of the relative clause.

e.g. **The man** (**who/that**) you spoke **to** is my assistant.

whose is used for possessive ideas.

e.g. **The woman whose responsibility** it is to check the invoices is off today. (*It's* ***the woman's*** *responsibility ...*)
That's the company whose employees went on strike last week. (*The company's employees went on strike ...*)

where refers to places.

e.g. **The hotel where** we used to stay has closed down.
I put it in **a place where** I thought it would be safe.

15 QUESTIONS AND NEGATIVES

15.1 Direct and indirect questions

In indirect questions and statements the question word(s) are not at the beginning of the sentence. We do not use *do/does/did* and the word order is normal sentence word order, i.e. subject-verb.

- *wh-* questions

Direct:		When **does** the flight **arrive**?
Indirect:	Do you know	when the flight **arrives**?
Direct:		When **will** it **be** ready?
Indirect:	Could you tell me	when it **will be** ready?
Direct:		How much **is** it?
Indirect:	I've got no idea	how much it **is**.

- *yes/no* questions
  We use *if/whether*.

Direct:		**Do** we **have** them in stock?
Indirect:	I'm not sure	**if/whether** we **have** them in stock.
Direct:		**Have** they **sent** an invoice?
Indirect:	Could you check	**if/whether** they **have sent** an invoice?
Direct:		**Is** there a swimming pool?
Indirect:	Don't forget to ask	**if/whether** there **is** a swimming pool.

15.2 Replying to negative sentences

When we want to confirm the correctness of a negative sentence, we use a negative.

e.g. – So you'**re not going** to the meeting?
– **No**, I'**m not**.

– You have**n't replied** yet (have you)?
– **No**, I **haven't**.

– So they **didn't cancel** the order?
– **No**, they **didn't**.

If we give a positive answer, it means the speaker is *not* correct. In this case we stress the auxiliary verb in the short answer and often add *actually*.

e.g. – So, you'**re not going** to the meeting?
– **Yes**, I ***am*** (actually).

– You have**n't replied** yet, **have** you?
– **Yes**, I ***have*** (actually).

– So, they **didn't cancel** the order?
– **Yes**, they ***did*** (actually).

16 LINKING IDEAS

16.1 Cause and effect

Note how we use *because, as* and *since* to link ideas where there is a cause–effect relationship.

e.g. All the hotels were full. (cause/reason)
We had to rent an apartment.(effect/consequence)

Because **Since** **As**	all the hotels were full, we had to rent apartment.

We had to rent an apartment	**because** **since** **as**	all the hotels were full.

Note the order of the two clauses can be changed. If we begin with *because/as/since*, there is a comma after the first clause.

We can also use *so* and *therefore* to link the two ideas but they cannot be at the beginning of the sentence.

e.g. All the hotels were full **so** we had to rent an apartment.
All the hotels were full. **Therefore** we had to rent an apartment.

Note there is a full stop before *therefore*. No punctuation is needed before *so*, although a comma is possible. *therefore* is more common in formal style.

due to/on account of/because of/as a result of can be used with noun phrases before reasons.

e.g. a lack of orders
(reason)
The company had to close down.
(consequence)

The company had to close down	**due to** **on account of** **because of** **as a result of**	a lack of orders.

The order of the clauses can be changed, with a comma separating the two clauses.

e.g. **As a result of a lack of** orders, the company had to close down.

16.2 Contrast

We use *although, even though* and *though* when there is a contrast between two ideas. This means that one idea is surprising in the light of another idea. They must be followed by a verb phrase (subject + verb).

e.g. Turnover has increased.
(a fact)Profits have fallen.
(this is surprising)

Although **Even though** **Though**	turnover has increased, (subject)	profits have fallen. (verb)

even though is more emphatic. The order of the two clauses can be changed.

e.g. Profits have fallen **even though** turnover has increased.

in spite of/despite are also used when ideas are in contrast but they need to be followed by a noun phrase. To do this we can add *the fact that* to a verb phrase.

e.g. **In spite** / **Despite** of the fact that turnover has increased, profits have fallen.
(not *In spite of turnover has increased …*)

The order of the clauses can be reversed.

e.g. Profits have fallen **in spite of the fact that** turnover has increased.

Sometimes we can add *-ing* to the verb to make a noun phrase.

e.g. **Despite arriving** at the airport late, we still managed to catch the flight.

Or we can use a noun.

e.g. My company is doing well **in spite of the recession**.
Despite the rain, we had a good holiday.

16.3 Sequencing

The following phrases can be used when describing a sequence (e.g. a process or the stages of a presentation):

First … First of all … To begin with … The first step is …
Second …
(And) Then … Next … After this/that … At this stage …
The next step is …
Before this/that …
(And) Finally …

Note *then* is not always the first word in the sentence.

e.g. These are **then** cut down into smaller lengths.
We will **then** have a look at our marketing strategies.

17 WORDS TO NOTE

17.1 *apparently, seem* and *appear*

apparently, seem and *appear* are used when we want to distance ourselves from information we are passing on. *apparently* is often used when we learn the information from another source (a person, the media, written records, etc.). *seem* and *appear* indicate that we may not be 100% sure of the correctness of a fact. They can all be used to create a polite style (especially when passing on negative news).

apparently usually goes at the beginning of a sentence.
e.g. **Apparently**, she's going to look for another job.
Apparently, there was a mistake on the invoice.

seem/appear can be used with *that*.
e.g. **It seems that** payment was never received.
It appears that the wrong order was sent out.

They can also be used with an infinitive (past or present).
e.g. We don't a**ppear to have received** your cheque.
There **seems to be/to have been** some sort of misunderstanding.

17.2 *average*

average can be used:

- as an adjective
  e.g. The **average temperature** is 24 degrees in summer months.
  These figures show **average monthly sales** per product area.
- as a noun
  e.g. **On average**, we spend £420 on stationery each month.
  What was **the average** for July?
  This is **a table of averages** for exports to Asian countries.
- as a verb
  e.g. **We average** over 4000 copies per week.
  Last year **turnover averaged** over £50,000 per month.

17.3 *be/get used to*

We use *be/get used to* when we want to indicate that something is a problem because we don't do it on a regular basis or that it isn't a problem because it is part of our normal routine. *be/get used to* must be followed by a noun phrase so we add *-ing* to a following verb.
e.g. I'**m used to getting up** early. (*So it's no problem for me.*)
I'**m not used to giving** presentations. (*So I will probably be nervous.*)
Are you **used to automatic cars**? (*Have you driven one before?*)

get has a more active meaning and is often used with *can't, couldn't, will have to, had to*.
e.g. You'**ll have to get used to driving** on the left when you go to the UK. (*In your country you drive on the right.*)
I **couldn't get used to working** nights. (*So I changed my job.*)
Are you **getting used to living** in a cold climate? (*Is it becoming easier for you?*)

Note that *used to* + infinitive is used for past habits or situations which are no longer true. There is no implication that something is or isn't a problem.
e.g. I **used to live** in Australia. (*But now I don't.*)

17.4 *had better*

We use *had better* (*not*) when we strongly recommend doing (or not doing) something in order to avoid a problem. *had better* is followed by an infinitive without *to*.
e.g. I'**d better give** him a call. (*It might be urgent.*)
You'**d better not say** anything. (*It could cause a problem.*)
Had I **better ring** and make a reservation? (*The restaurant may be busy.*)

Note also how it is used in short answers.
e.g. – Do you think I should let her know?
– Yes, you'**d better**.

– Should we postpone the meeting?
– No, we'**d better not**.

17.5 *like* and *as*

When we use *as* it indicates that what follows is a fact.
e.g. **As the manager**, it's my job to make difficult decisions.
(= Because I am the manager).
She **works as** a safety officer.
(= This is her job.)
The operation **was** originally **set up as** a joint venture.
(= It was a joint venture.)
This **is used as** an extra storeroom.
(= This is the function of the room.)
The changes are **as follows**.
(= They are shown below.)

like has more the meaning of *similar to*.
e.g. We **are not like** all the other PR companies.
(= We aren't similar to ...)
The banks **are run like** private companies.
(= But they aren't private companies.)
This **seems like** a very friendly place to work.
(= This is my impression.)

like can be used with verbs to mean *in the same way as*.
e.g. I **was shaking like** a leaf. (= I was very nervous.)

Note also *look like*.
e.g. What does your briefcase **look like**? (= Describe it.)

17.6 *look/sound as if/though*

look as if/though and *sound as if/though* can be used to mean *seem*. *sound as if* is usually used when someone has told you something.
e.g. It **looks as though** we're not going to achieve our targets this year.
You **look as if** you need a good rest.
It **sounds as if** you had a really good time.

17.7 *make* and *do*

The basic meaning of *make* is to produce or create.

e.g. We **make** jet engines.
I'**m making** some coffee.

make is also used to talk about appointments.

e.g. Can you **make** the 17th?

do has a more general meaning related to activities:

e.g. What **are** you **doing** this evening?
What **does** your company **do**?
She's **doing** the end-of-year accounts.

Note the following expressions:

make a decision	do well/badly
make plans	do better/worse
make money	do something about
make a loss/a profit	do some work
make an offer	do business with
make progress	do your best
make an effort	do someone a favour
make a complaint	do the talking

17.8 *myself, ourselves, my/our own*

myself	ourselves
yourself	yourselves
himself/herself/itself	themselves
my own	our own
your own	your own
his/her/its	own their own

Note how we use these to emphasise who does something.

e.g. I make all **my** travel arrangements **myself**.
I make all **my own** travel arrangements.
We do **our** advertising **ourselves**.
We do **our own** advertising.
Do you have to do **your** typing **yourself/yourselves**?
Do you have to do **your own** typing?

We also use *myself*, etc. when the subject and the object of a sentence are the same.

e.g. **I** burnt **myself** on the photocopier. (not *I burnt me*)
Could **you** introduce **yourselves**?

17.9 *rather than*

rather than means *instead of/and not*. It is used when we are talking about two options.

e.g. I think we should go by train **rather than drive**.
She usually goes **by train rather than (by) bus**.
It would be better to start at **9 rather than 10**.

17.10 *say, tell* and *ask*

Note the following structures with *say, tell* and *ask*.

say (+ noun) (+ *to* + someone) (*about* + something)

e.g. Did he **say**?
Did she **say anything to you about it**?
(not *Can you say me…*)

say + (*that*)

e.g. Did he **say (that)** he was coming?

say + *if/whether*

e.g. Did she **say if/whether** they'd received the order?

Note we use *say* when we are referring to something that is written.

e.g. It **says/said** in the report that …

tell + noun/pronoun (*about* + *something*) or (+ infinitive)

e.g. Did you **tell her about it**?
Can you **tell her to come** before 6?

tell + noun/pronoun + (*that*)

e.g. Could you **tell him (that)** Jose called?
(not *Could you tell that Jose called?*)

ask + noun/pronoun

e.g. I'd like to **ask something**.

ask + noun/pronoun + infinitive

e.g. Can you **ask him to call** me?
(not *Can you ask to him to call?*)

ask (+ noun/pronoun) + *if/whether*

e.g. Did you **ask (them) if/whether** they are coming?

17.11 *so* and *such (a)*

so and *such* are used to add emphasis.

We use *so* before adjectives without nouns.

e.g. It was ***so* expensive**.

so is also used before *much, many, few* and *little*.

e.g. We're under **so much** pressure at the moment.
I've got **so many** things to do.
There were **so few** people there.
We had **so little** time.

We use *such a(n)* before an adjective and a singular countable noun, and *such* before an adjective and an uncountable noun or a countable plural.

e.g. It's **such a** fast **machine**.
It was **such an** awful **flight**.
I wasn't expecting **such** terrible **weather**.
They are **such** good **customers**.

We also use *such* before a *lot* (*of*):

e.g. I've got **such a lot of** work to do.

Sometimes *so* and *such* are followed by a *that* clause to give a consequence.

e.g. They offer **such** good deals **that** it's difficult to compete with them.
We had **so** many orders **that** we had to take on more staff.

17.12 *speak* and *talk*

speak is used for languages, in telephone phrases and for the physical act of speaking.

e.g. Can I **speak to** Sarah, please?
She **speaks** fluent Chinese.
Could you **speak** a bit more slowly, please?

talk is used more for conversation and discussion.

e.g. Who were you **talking to**?
What did you **talk about**?
She **talks** a lot.
Have you got time **to talk**?

talk can be used to introduce a presentation.

e.g. Today I'd like t**o talk to you about** ...

Sometimes we can use either.

e.g. I'll need to **speak/talk** to my boss about it.

17.13 *still, yet* and *already*

still is used when we want to emphasise that a situation may be continuing. It is used with present tenses and the Present Perfect, and can be used in affirmatives, negatives and questions.

e.g. I'm **still working** for the same company.
I'm afraid I **still haven't finished** it.
Do you **still drive** a Volvo?

yet and *already* are used to mean *before this time/by now*.

yet is used with questions and negatives. It is used with the Present Simple and Present Perfect (the Past Simple is possible in US English).

e.g. I **haven't finished** it **yet**.
Have you **done** it **yet**?
I'**m not** ready **yet**.

Note the link between *yet* and *still*.

e.g. – **Have** you **finished** the report yet?
– No, **I'm still working** on it.

already is used with affirmative sentences. It is used with the Present Perfect (the Past Simple is possible in US English).

e.g. I'**ve already sent** confirmation.

17.14 *such as, like* and *for example*

such as and *like* can be used to give examples of a preceding noun.

e.g. **Companies such as/like IBM**, for example, have a huge turnover.
I would love to live in a hot country **such as/like Thailand**.

such as and *like* can also be followed by *this/these* to mean *this type of*.

e.g. In **a situation such as/like this** ...
We can save a lot of time using **methods such as/like these**.

Note when the example is in a separate sentence, we have to use *for example*.

e.g. There are various ways of paying. **For example**, you can pay by bank transfer.

17.15 *too* and *enough*

too + adjective or adverb is used in a negative sense (unlike *very*, which just strengthens the meaning of an adjective or adverb).

e.g. It's **too hot** in here.
This chair is **too high** for me.

We often use *too* with *for* + person + infinitive to state what the problem is.

e.g. The text on the overhead was **too small for people to read**.
She speaks **too fast for me to follow** her.

Adjective/adverb + *enough* is used to talk about how acceptable something is in a certain way. *enough* can also be used with *for* + person + infinitive.

e.g. Is this room **big enough** to hold the meeting in?
I didn't read the small print **carefully enough**.

enough + noun refers to the sufficiency of something.

e.g. Have we got **enough petrol**?
There wasn't **enough space for me to park**.

17.16 *while, during, in, for* and *since*

during is used with a noun for a period of time in which something happens.

e.g. She would like to visit the factory **during** her stay.
We employ a lot of casual staff **during** the summer.
I can never sleep **during** a flight.

in is used with months, seasons, years, etc.

e.g. I usually take my holiday **in** the autumn.

while is used with a verb phrase for a period of time in which something happens.

e.g. I'll still be able to pick up my emails **while** I'm away.
Did you see Yu Ling **while** you were in Beijing?
I didn't see much of France **while** I was working there.

Note we could also use *when*.

for is used with lengths of time and *since* with a point of time (in the past).

e.g. I haven't seen him **since** last August / **for** six months.
I worked for them **for** five years.
He's away **for** three weeks.

17.17 *would prefer/would rather*

would prefer and *would rather* are used to talk about preferences for a specific occasion. They are often used when making and responding to invitations. They can both be followed by nouns. With verbs, *prefer* is followed by *to* + infinitive; *would rather* is just followed by an infinitive.

e.g. What **would** you **rather do**?
Would you **prefer to go** to an Italian or Chinese restaurant?
Would you **rather** a cold drink?
Would you **rather not go** out?

I'**d prefer** a non-smoking room.
I'**d prefer to go** to the cinema.
I'**d rather not stay** too late.
He'**d prefer not to stay** overnight.

18 FUNCTIONAL LANGUAGE

18.1 Requests

Spoken requests:

Can/could I make a booking?	Yes, of course. /
Could/would you give me a hand (please)?	No problem.
Could/would you (please) not say anything?	
Could he/she call me on this number?	
Would you mind giving me a lift?	No, of course
Would you mind not smoking (please)?	not. / No problem.

Written requests:

please often goes before or immediately after *could/would*.
e.g. **Please could/would** you send me a copy of your latest brochure.
Could/would you **please** look into this matter.

We can also use:
Please let me know as soon as possible.
I **would** be (very) grateful if you **could** call me.

18.2 Offers

Offering something:

Can/could I get you something to drink?

Yes, I'd love a coffee.	No, I'm fine thanks.

Offering to do something:

Shall I open the window?	Yes, please. It's very hot in here. If you don't mind, I'd rather you didn't.
Would you like me to send you a copy?	Yes, please. No, it's OK. I've already got one.
Let me help you.	Thanks very much. It's OK thanks. I can manage.

18.3 Suggestions and advice

Suggestions involving the speaker:

Let's fix up an appointment.
Shall we meet in the bar?
How about (going for) a drink later?
We could meet another time.
Why don't we go to an Italian restaurant?
I think we should catch an earlier flight.

Suggestions to another person:

Why don't you go home?
Why not give him a call?
Have you thought of taking them to a show?
Have you tried switching it off?
I would recommend taking the motorway.
You could organise a welcoming party.
I suggest (that) you try again later.

Advice:

(I think) you should have a word with your boss.
I don't think you should resign.
Do you think we should change the venue?
If I were you, I'd/I wouldn't ring her.
You'd/we'd better (not) postpone the meeting.
It's best/a good idea to take a small gift.
It's best/a good idea not to drink the tap water.
Make sure you check all the equipment.
Make sure you don't leave anything behind.
(You should/must) always leave a tip in the States.
(You should/must) never arrive late.

Reporting suggestions and advice:

He suggested that we meet later this month.
She advised us to consult a lawyer.
He advised me not to say anything.

18.4 Apologies

Making apologies:

Sorry I'm late.
I'm sorry to interrupt you but …
I'm sorry (that) I wasn't here when you arrived.
We are very sorry about the delay.
We would like to apologise for any inconvenience caused.
I apologise for not having replied earlier.
We regret to inform you that we have had to cancel the conference.

Accepting apologies:

That's okay. / Don't worry about it.
It's not a problem. / Never mind.
It really doesn't matter.
There's really no need to apologise.

Rejecting apologies:

I wish you'd let me know.
You should/could have sent me an email.
I'm sorry. It just isn't good enough.
Please make sure that it doesn't happen again.

18.5 Agreement and disagreement

Strong agreement:	**Agreement:**
Absolutely!	I agree (with that/you).
I totally agree.	We're in agreement on that.
I couldn't agree more.	I'm in favour of the plan.
	That's right.

Mild agreement:
You may be right.
I suppose that's true.
I agree with you up to a point.
I agree with most of what you say.

Mild disagreement:
Yes, but ...
That's not necessarily true.
I'm not sure I agree.

Disagreement:
I don't agree with that.
I'm opposed to spending any more money.

Strong disagreement:
I disagree completely.
I totally disagree.
That isn't true.

18.6 Opinions

Asking for opinions:
What do you think?
What do you think of the new marketing manager? (*of* + person/thing)
What do you think about the proposed cuts? (*about* + situation)
What's your opinion/view (on this)?
Do you agree with me?
Do you consider it's worth doing?

Giving opinions:
I (don't) think it's a good idea.
In my opinion/view ...
I reckon ...

---

19 IRREGULAR VERBS

Infinitive	Past tense	Past participle
be	was	been
become	became	become
begin	began	begun
bend	bent	bent
bite	bit	bitten
blow	blew	blown
break	broke	broken
bring	brought	brought
build	built	built
burn	burnt	burnt
buy	bought	bought
can	could/was able	been able
catch	caught	caught
choose	chose	chosen
come	came	come
cost	cost	cost
cut	cut	cut
do	did	done
draw	drew	drawn
drink	drank	drunk
drive	drove	driven
eat	ate	eaten
fall	fell	fallen
feed	fed	fed
feel	felt	felt
fight	fought	fought
find	found	found
fly	flew	flown
forecast	forecast	forecast
forget	forgot	forgotten
get	got	got
give	gave	given

Infinitive	Past tense	Past participle
go	went	gone
grow	grew	grown
have	had	had
hear	heard	heard
hit	hit	hit
hold	held	held
hurt	hurt	hurt
keep	kept	kept
know	knew	known
lay	laid	laid
lead	led	led
learn	learnt/ learned	learnt/ learned
leave	left	left
lend	lent	lent
let	let	let
lie	lay	lain
lose	lost	lost
make	made	made
mean	meant	meant
meet	met	met
pay	paid	paid
put	put	put
read	read	read
ride	rode	ridden
ring	rang	rung
rise	rose	risen
run	ran	run
say	said	said
see	saw	seen
sell	sold	sold
send	sent	sent
set	set	set

Infinitive	Past tense	Past participle
shake	shook	shaken
shine	shone	shone
show	showed	shown
shut	shut	shut
sing	sang	sung
sit	sat	sat
sleep	slept	slept
smell	smelt	smelt
speak	spoke	spoken
spell	spelt	spelt
spend	spent	spent
stand	stood	stood

Infinitive	Past tense	Past participle
steal	stole	stolen
swim	swam	swum
take	took	taken
teach	taught	taught
tell	told	told
think	thought	thought
throw	threw	thrown
understand	understood	understood
wake up	woke up	woken up
wear	wore	worn
win	won	won
write	wrote	written

20 VERB FORMS

Affirmative	Negative	Interrogative	Short answer
Present Simple			
I/you/we/they work. He/she/it works.	I/you/we/they don't (do not) work. He/she/it doesn't (does not) work.	Do you/we/they work? Does he/she/it work?	Yes, I/you/we/they do. Yes, he/she/it does. No, I/you/we/they don't. No, he/she/it doesn't.
Present Continuous			
I'm (I am), you/we/they're (they are) working. He/she/it isn't (is not) working.	I'm, you/we/ they're not (you/we/they aren't) working. He/she/it isn't (he/she/it's not) working.	Am I, you/we/they working? Is he/she/it working?	Yes, I am, you/we/they are. Yes, he/she/it is. No, I'm not. No, you/we/they aren't.
***going to*: Future**			
I'm, you/we/ they're going to work. He/she/it's going to work.	I'm, you/we/ they're not going to work. He/she/it isn't going to work.	Am I, are you/we/they going to work? Is it/he/she going to work?	Yes, I am. Yes, you/we/they are. Yes, he/she/it isn't. No, I'm not. No, you/we/they aren't. No, he/she/it isn't.
***will*: Future**			
I/you/we/they'll (they will) work. He/she/it'll (it will) work.	I/you/we/they won't (will not) work. He/she/it won't work.	Will I/you/they work? Will he/she/it work?	Yes, I/you/we/they will. Yes, he/she/it will. No, I/you/we/they won't. No, he/she/it won't.

20 VERB FORMS continued

Affirmative	Negative	Interrogative	Short answer
Future Continuous			
I/you/we/they'll (they will) be working. He/she/it'll (it will) be working.	I/you/we/they won't be working. He/she/it won't be working.	Will I/you/we/they be working? Will he/she/it be working?	Yes, I/you/we/they will. Yes, he/she/it will. No, I/you/we/they won't. No, he/she/it won't.
Past Simple			
I/you/we/they worked. He/she/it worked.	I/you/we/they didn't (did not) work. He/she/it didn't work.	Did I/you/we/they work? Did he/she/it work?	Yes, I/you/we/they did. Yes, he/she/it did. No, I/you/we/they didn't. No, he/she/it didn't.
Past Continuous			
I was working. You/we/they were working. He/she/it was working.	I wasn't (was not) working. You/we/they weren't (were not) working. He/she/it wasn't working.	Was I working? Were you/we/they working? Was he/she/it working?	Yes, I was. Yes, you/we/they were. Yes, he/she/it was. No, I wasn't. No, you/we/they weren't. No, he/she/it wasn't.
Present Perfect			
I/you/we/they've (they have) worked. He/she/it's (it has) worked.	I/you/we/they haven't (have not) worked. He/she/it hasn't (has not) worked.	Have I/you/we/ they worked? Has he/she/it worked?	Yes, I/you/we/they have. Yes, he/she/it has. No, I/you/we/they haven't. No, he/she/it hasn't.
Present Perfect Continuous			
I/you/we/they've (they have) been working. He/she/it's (it has) been working.	I/you/we/they haven't been working. He/she/it hasn't been working.	Have I/you/we/ they been working? Has he/she/it been working?	Yes, I/you/we/they have. Yes, he/she/it has. No, I/you/we/they haven't. No, he/she/it hasn't.

---

21 USEFUL INFORMATION

21.1 Numbers

Fractions and decimals:

$^1/_4$ = a/one-quarter
$^3/_4$ = three-quarters
$^2/_3$ = two-thirds
$^4/_5$ = four-fifths
$^1/_2$ = a half
$^1/_3$ = a/one-third
$^1/_5$ = a/one-fifth
.5 = point five

4.07 = four point oh (or zero) seven
23.685 = twenty-three point six eight five

High numbers:

100,000	a/one hundred thousand
150,000	a/one hundred and fifty thousand
23,500,000	twenty-three million five hundred thousand
250,000	a quarter of a million; two hundred and fifty thousand
500,000	half a million; five hundred thousand
750,000	three-quarters of a million; seven hundred and fifty thousand
3,250,000	three and a quarter million; three point two five million; three million two hundred and fifty thousand
3.75m	three and three-quarter million; three point seven five million; three million seven hundred and fifty thousand
2.5bn	two and a half billion; two point five billion
5.82bn	five point eight two billion

Abbreviations:
20k = twenty thousand   70m = seventy million
2bn = two billion

Notes

1 The point (.) is used to show decimals. The comma (,) is used to show thousands or millions or billions.
2 We put *and* after hundred(s). We only put *and* after thousand(s) if there are no hundreds.
3 After the decimal point we say numbers individually.
4 0 can be *oh, nought* or *zero*.
5 One in front of *million, thousand* or *hundred* can be *one* or *a*.
6 *Hundred, thousand, million* and *billion* are usually in the singular when used with a number.

21.2 Symbols and mathematical terms

Reference numbers:
/ = stroke or slash (US)
– = dash or hyphen
e.g. 407/ZX-1 (= four oh seven stroke Z X dash one)

Mathematical symbols and terms:

+	plus	#	hash
–	minus/less	@	at
×	times, multiplied by	50-50	fifty fifty
÷	divided by	1:3	one to three
=	equals		
%	per cent ($17^1/_2$% = seventeen and a half per cent)		

$200–$300 two to three hundred dollars; between two hundred and three hundred dollars

21.3 Measurements and dimensions

Imperial and metric equivalent measurements:
1 inch (in) = 2.54 centimetres (cm)
1 foot (ft) = 0.305 metres (m)
1 mile (m) = 1.609 kilometres (km)
1 ounce (oz) = 28.35 grams (g)
1 pound (lb) = 0.454 kilograms (kg)
1 pint (pt) = 0.568 litres (l)
1 gallon (gal) = 4.54 litres

Dimensions:

5m × 4m	five metres by four metres
$10m^2$/10sq	ten square metres
$10cm^3$/10cu cm	ten cubic centimetres

Note:
The pipe is two metres long/in length.
It's a two-metre long pipe. (not *two metres long*)
The sheet is 40cms wide/in width/across.
It's 2cms in diameter.

21.4 The time

Saying the time:
A simple way to say the time is to say the numbers.
e.g. 9.30 (= nine thirty)
10.57 (= ten fifty-seven)
11.04 (= eleven oh four)

To say the hours:
10.00   ten   ten o'clock

To be more precise:

ten in the morning	10am	(am = midnight to midday)
ten in the evening	10pm	(pm = midday to midnight)

We can also say:
11.05 five past eleven
11.08 eight minutes past eleven
11.15 a quarter past eleven
11.30 half past eleven
11.35 twenty-five to twelve
11.45 a quarter to twelve

2.20 = twenty past two in British English; twenty after two in American English.
2.55 = five to three in British English; five of three in American English.

The 24 hour clock:

12.00	twelve hundred hours
1pm / 13.00	thirteen hundred hours
3.30pm / 15.30	fifteen thirty

Talking about time differences:
We're two hours behind you.
They're ten hours ahead of us.
That's eight in the morning New York time.
Five in the afternoon your time is eleven in the morning our time.
That's 4.30 local time.
We're on GMT (Greenwich Mean Time).
They're on Eastern Standard Time.
Have you moved your clocks forward/back yet?

21.5 Geographical areas

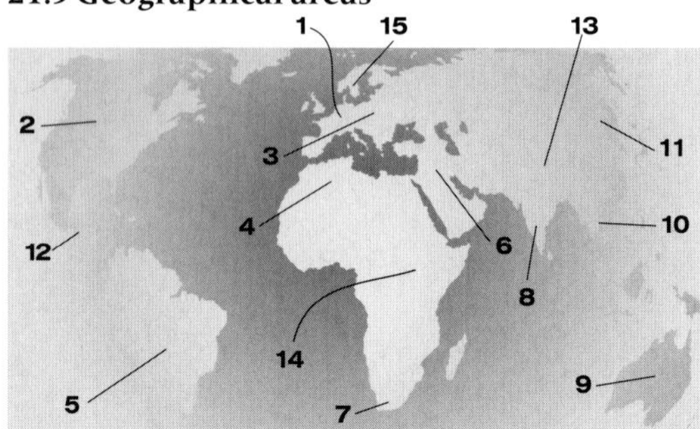

1 Western Europe
2 North America
3 Eastern Europe
4 North Africa
5 South America
6 Middle East
7 Southern Africa
8 India/South Asia
9 Australia
10 South-East Asia
11 Far East/Asia Pacific
12 Central America
13 Central Asia
14 East Africa
15 Scandinavia

The names for different regions of the world can vary depending on where you live.

21.6 Abbreviations and acronyms

There are many abbreviations and acronyms (where the initials of a word or name are used). Some are widely used; some are used only within one industry, one company or even one department of a company. The list that follows includes many abbreviations that are widely used.

a/c	account
AGM	annual general meeting
AOB	any other business
ASEAN	Association of South East Asian Nations
att/attn	(for the) attention (of)
bal	balance
b/f	bring/brought forward
cc	copies to
CEO	chief executive officer
encl/enc	enclosed
EGM	extraordinary general meeting
ETA	estimated time of arrival
EU	European Union
GDP	gross domestic product
i.e.	that is/in other words (*id est*)
IMF	International Monetary Fund
inc	incorporated
IT	information technology
MD	managing director
NATO	North Atlantic Treaty Organisation
NB	note/take special note of (*nota bene*)
OPEC	Organisation of Petroleum Exporting Countries
o/s	outstanding
PA	personal assistant
PC	personal computer
PLC	public limited company
pp	on behalf of
PR	public relations
PTO	please turn over
R&D	research and development
re	regarding/in connection with
ref	reference/with reference to
RPI	retail price index
UN	United Nations
VAT	value-added tax
WHO	World Health Organization

21.7 Notes on verb contractions

In speech and in formal writing, some verb forms are contracted with:

- personal pronouns: *I'm* (I am), *they've* (they have), etc.
- question words: *What's* (What is), *How'll* (How will), etc.
- demonstrative pronouns: *that's* (that is), *these're* (these are), etc.
- there: *there's* (there is), *there'd be* (there would be), etc.

Contracted forms are not used in affirmative short answers:

Yes, I am. (not *Yes, I'm.*)
Yes, they have. (not *Yes, they've.*)

However, they are used in negative short answers:
No, we don't.
No, she can't.

The following contracted forms are used in this book:

is/are
I'm (I am), *he/she/it's* (he/she/it is), *there's* (there is), *What's* (What is), *Where's* (Where is), *that's* (that is), *these're* (these are), *isn't* (is not), *we/you/they're* (we/you/they are), *there're* (there are), *aren't* (are not).

was/were
wasn't (was not), *weren't* (were not)

has/have
he/she/it's (he/she/it has), *I/we/you/they've* (I/we/you/they have), *hasn't* (has not), *haven't* (have not)

do/did
don't (do not), *didn't* (did not)

will/can
I/you/he'll (I/you/he will), *won't* (will not), *can't* (cannot)

would/must/could/should
I/we/you/she'd (I/we/you/she would), *wouldn't* (would not), *couldn't* (could not), *shouldn't* (should not)

Glossary of business-related terms

acquisition: acquiring something; in business this is usually another company, e.g. *XYZ plc is our latest acquisition*
ad hoc: an ad hoc meeting is a meeting arranged informally to suit the participants
AGM: annual general meeting
Annual Percentage Rate (APR): rate of interest (such as on hire-purchase agreements) shown on an annual compound basis, including fees and charges
annual report: report of a company's financial situation at the end of each year, sent to all shareholders
anti-trust: attacks monopolies and encourages competition
AOB: Any Other Business (on an agenda)
APR: annual percentage rate (see above)
Arabic numerals: numbers written as 1, 2, 3, 4, etc. (see also Roman numerals)
assets: things which belong to a company or person, and which have a realistic value
asset value: value of a company calculated by adding together all its assets (see also current assets and fixed assets)
audit: examination of the books and accounts of a company
authorisation: give formal approval; sanction something
back-up: support
balance: amount to be put in one of the columns of an account to make the total debits and credits equal
balance brought forward/carried forward: amount entered in an account at the end of a period or page of an account book to balance the debit and credit entries; it is then taken forward to start the new period or page
balance sheet: statement of the financial position of a company at a particular time
beamer: a digital projector
bid: offering an amount of money for something in competition with other people/organisations; the highest bidder is successful in securing the goods or services
(the) book (financial jargon): the value of an asset according to the company's books/accounts
bought ledger: set of accounts recording money owed to each supplier, i.e. the creditors of the company
branch: local office or shop belonging to a larger organisation
brand: the make/name of a product
broker: dealer who acts as a middleman between a buyer and a seller (stock broker: person who buys or sells shares for clients; insurance broker: person who sells insurance to clients)
budget: plan of expected spending and income (usually for one year)
bullet points: a list of points identified by dots or asterisks
buyout (management buyout): takeover of a company by a group of employees (usually managers and directors)
capital: the money put into a business
capital goods: goods used to manufacture other goods, i.e. machinery
carry forward: to take an account balance at the end of the current period as the starting point for the next period (see also balance)
catalogue selling: selling from a book where items for sale are listed
catering: providing food and drink for a number of people
CBI: Confederation of British Industries
CEO: chief executive officer
chartered accountant: accountant who has passed professional examinations and is a member of the Institute of Chartered Accountants
commission: financial proportion of a sale paid to the person who makes the sale, e.g. 5% of total value of sales
company secretary: role of administrative responsibility within an organisation
conglomerate: group of subsidiary companies linked together and forming a group, each making very different types of products
contract out: the company gives a proportion of its work to an outside organisation or person; this may be because the work contracted out requires skills not provided by the company, or because the company is too busy
conveyancing: legally transferring a property from a seller to a buyer
core business: main business
credit control: check that customers pay on time and do not owe more than their credit limit
credit limit: fixed amount which is the most a customer can owe in credit
creditor: organisation/business/person owed money
current assets: assets used by a company in its ordinary work (such as materials, finished products, cash, monies due) and which are held for a short time only
customise: change to fit the special needs of a customer
cut down on: reduce
CV: curriculum vitae; a summary of a person's work experience and education/qualifications
defer (deferred taxation): to put back to a later date or to postpone
depreciation: reduction in value of an asset
diversification: taking on forms of work that are different, but related to, the core business of the organisation/company
dividend: percentage of profits paid to shareholders
equity: value of a company's shares
estimate: an approximation rather than something precise or specific
ETA: estimated time of arrival
expenditure: the total financial outgoings (spending) of a company/business
expressway (UK English motorway): a stretch of road with three or more lanes of traffic going in the same direction; there may be a payment for travelling on these roads
factoring: business of buying debt at a discount (a 'factor' collects a company's debts when due, and pays the creditor in advance part of the sum to be collected, so 'buying' the debt)

(to) fire: to tell someone that you no longer need him/her to work for the company,e.g. *We had to fire him because he just wasn't meeting our requirements*
fire retardant: chemical which slows down the burning process
fiscal: referring to tax or to government revenues
fiscal year: 12-month period on which taxes are calculated, e.g. in the UK 6 April to the following 5 April
fixed assets: property or machinery which a company owns and uses, but which the company does not buy and sell as part of its regular trade, including the company's investments in shares or other companies
flagship: something of importance, e.g. *The paper-shredder is our flagship product*
flipchart: a board with paper attached
franchise: licence to trade using a brand name and paying a royalty for it
franchising: act of selling a licence to trade as a franchise
freehold site: site which the owner holds forever and on which no rent is paid
freelance: an independent worker who works for several different companies
fringe benefits: extra items given by a company to workers in addition to a salary, e.g. company cars, private health insurance
GDP: gross domestic product
GNP: gross national product
goodwill: adding value beyond money alone, e.g. *The company has built up goodwill because of the fair way it treats its customers*
gross profit: profit before deductions (e.g. tax)
hand over to: give time/responsibility to someone else
hard disk: computer disk which has a sealed case and can store large quantities of information
hardware: computer hardware; machines used in data processing including the computers and printer, but not the programs
hedge: protecting yourself against a loss (possibly financial), e.g. *a hedge against inflation*
human resources: the workers a company has available, seen from the point of view of their skills and experience
Inc. (US): incorporated
inflation: an increase in prices
institutional investors: institutions such as pension funds and insurance companies that buy large quantities of shares
intangible assets: the value of something that isn't physical, e.g. a trademark
interest: payment made by a borrower for the use of money, calculated as a percentage of the capital borrowed (high interest = interest at a high percentage)
interest rate: percentage charge for borrowing money
investment trust: company whose shares can be brought on the Stock Exchange, and whose business is to make money by buying and selling stocks and shares
joint venture: very large business project where two companies join together, often forming a new joint company to manage the project
lease: an agreement (generally for a fixed period and a fixed amount of money) between someone who owns something and someone who wants to rent it
ledger: book in which accounts are written
liabilities: debts of a business
liaise: communicate about something; meet in a specific place
license: to give someone official permission to do something
licensee: person who has a licence, especially a licence to sell alcohol or to manufacture something
logistics: the practicalities of a chain of events, e.g. getting materials shipped from one country to another so they can be used in a factory to make finished goods, which are then forwarded to retail outlets
loss adjuster: person who calculates how much insurance should be paid on a claim
margin: difference between the money received when selling a product and the money paid for it
margins: profit margins
market: area where products might be sold, or group of people who might buy a product
market leader: company with the largest market share
market value: value of a product or company if sold today
materials handling: moving raw materials and semi-finished goods from one place to another
MD: managing director
merchant bank: bank which arranges loans to companies and deals in international finance, buys and sells shares, launches new companies on the Stock Exchange, but does not provide normal banking services to the general public
motion: a formal proposal put forward at a meeting
net: price, weight or pay, etc. after all deductions have been made
net profit: profit after deductions (e.g. tax)
network: system which links different points together
NIC: national insurance contributions
offering: a contribution
off-the-shelf: ready-made
operating cost: costs of the day-to-day organisation of a company
operating profit: profits made by a company in its usual business
O/S: outstanding; not yet paid or completed
outsource: to give work to another company/person outside the company
overdraft: when a person/organisation has spent more money than is in their bank account
PA: personal assistant
parent company: company which owns more than 50% of the shares of another company
partnership: unregistered business where two or more people (but not more than 20) share the risks and profits according to a partnership scheme
passive smoking: breathing in other people's cigarette/pipe/cigar smoke
petty cash: a float of cash kept in an office to cover general and day-to-day expenses
PIN (personal identification number): unique number allocated to the holder of a cash or credit card, by which the holder can enter an automatic banking system
PLC (UK): public limited company
PR: public relations
pre-dyed: colour-dyed before

premises: a building for either staff or goods, e.g. *Our warehouse premises are where we keep the bulk of our goods*
president: head of a company; in the UK, president is sometimes a title given to a non-executive former chairman of a company; in the USA, the president is the main executive director of a company
products: range of products = different products from which a customer can choose; a line of products = different products that form a group (a range of products might include a number of different lines)
profit and loss account: statement of a company's expenditure and income over a period of time, almost always one calendar year, showing whether that company has made a profit or loss
proofs: test copies of written materials
proprietor: owner (see also sole trader)
protectionism: protecting producers in the home country against foreign competitors by banning or taxing imports or by imposing import quotas
prototype: the first model of new machine, built for testing
proviso: a condition
publicly owned: the company's shares are owned by the public and can be traded on the Stock Exchange
quantity surveyor: person who carries out a quantity survey (to carry out a quantity survey = to estimate the amount of materials and the cost of the labour required for a construction project)
query: a doubt or uncertainty about something, e.g. *I have a query on this invoice; Can I query that date with you?*
ratify: to give formal consent or approval, e.g. *Management have ratified the new contracts for factory workers*
receipt: a document to prove purchase of goods or services, e.g. *Make sure you get a receipt when you pay the taxi fare*
recruitment: finding new people to join a company
redundancy: being no longer employed, because the job is no longer necessary
redundancy package: various benefits and payments given to a worker who is being made redundant
reimburse: to give money back for services and goods already paid for, e.g. *Will you reimburse me for the train fare?; These goods are faulty, so I'd like you to reimburse the total costs*
retail outlets: shops
retail sales: sales to the general public
revenue: income
Roman numerals: numbers written as i, ii, iii, iv, etc. (see also Arabic numerals)
RPI: retail price index = index which shows how prices of consumer goods have increased or decreased over a period of time
search engine: a computer program that locates information; Google and Yahoo! are Internet search engines
securities: investments in stock and shares; certificates to show that someone owns stocks or shares
server: a computer program that links the user to data, e.g. a web server provides documents to your computer from the World Wide Web
settlement: an agreement, usually financial, e.g. *ABC Ltd made a huge out-of-court settlement*
sewage plant: a place where waste matter is treated
(on the) shop floor: in the factory, in the works or among the ordinary workers
Sir/Lord (UK): honorary titles
sole proprietor: person who owns a business on his own, with no partners, without forming a company
sole trader: person who runs a business by himself but has not registered it as a company
spreadsheet: a document on which financial information is kept, e.g. *Can we see the spreadsheet for last month's sales?*
stifle: to suppress or control something
stock: materials to be used in production or goods to be sold
stock market: stock exchange, a trading and dealing house
stocks and shares: shares in ordinary companies
(to) subcontract: to agree with an outside company that they will do part of the work for a project
subcontractor: company which has a contract to do work for a main contractor
subscription: a sum of money paid for membership of a club or for delivery of newspapers, journals, etc.
subsistence allowance: money provided by an employer which is designed to cover basic living costs and expenses
sundry expenses: various small expenses which are not itemised
systems analysis: using a computer to suggest how a company should work by analysing the way in which it works at present
systems analyst: persons who specialises in systems analysis
takeover: the purchase of a controlling interest in one company by another company
tally: correspond with, match, e.g. *We managed to get the final figures to tally*
tender (to put a job out to tender): to invite an outside company to bid for the work
'top-drawer': expression meaning 'first class'
trim: decorative detail
turnover: total amount of goods/services sold by a company
turnpike: see expressway
Twh: the terawatt hour, a unit for measuring energy; it corresponds to 1,000,000,000 kWh (kilowatt hours)
utility company: company that is regulated by its own country to provide a public service, e.g. the Swedish company Vattenfall provides energy in Europe under government control
value-added tax (US equivalent 'sales tax'): tax imposed as a percentage of the invoice value of goods and services
VAT: value-added tax
waiver: giving up (a right) or removing the conditions (of a rule)
waiver clause: clause in a contract giving the conditions under which the rights in the contract can be given up
weblink: a link that takes you from one part of the World Wide Web to another
weighting (regional weighting allowance): additional salary or wages paid to compensate for living in an expensive part of the country
weld: to join two pieces of metal together by melting the parts which touch each other
works manager: person in charge of a works/plant
write off: to cancel an outstanding debt or to acknowledge a failure of some kind, e.g. *At the G8 summit, politicians met to discuss writing off third world debt; The last idea was a complete write off, so we're going to start again!*

Answers

UNIT 1 Everyday business contacts

1 **a** The Swedish financial controller uses English on a daily basis. She has some problems when using English on the phone.
b The Chilean clerk needs English mainly for his written work (checking documents, etc.). He has some problems with his written English.

2 **1** **a** Is that
b got a minute
c Go ahead
2 **d** Are you busy?
e three o'clock your time
f to you later
3 **g** we covered everything
h tell him I called
i give him the message

3 **a** *the* for a famous bearer of a name.
c i as a patient; ii as a visitor
f No difference.
All others: *the* for specific references; *a*/*an* for unspecific references.

4 **a** some / (–) **b** some
c the **d** –
e a **f** –
g an **h** the

UNIT 2 Developing contacts

1 **a** False **b** False
c False **d** True
e True

2 **a** so **b** few
c much **d** such
e many **f** little
g so **h** few

3 **a** reliable; hard working
b efficient **c** energetic
d likeable **e** friendly
f highly qualified **g** outgoing
h cheerful; competent

4 **e** Hello.
f Hello. Yes?
b Can I speak to Carla Vito, please?
k Who? What was the name?
c Carla Vito. That's V-I-T-O.
d Excuse me, but do you know what the time is?
i Am I too late? Is the office closed?
h It's four o'clock in the morning.
j Oh. I thought you were six hours behind us.
a And it's Labor Day. Nobody works today.
g OK, I'll be in touch tomorrow. Sorry to disturb you.

5 **a** eighteen months ago
b three months ago
c a couple of months ago
d in a fortnight / in two weeks
e in three months' time
f the other day
g last year
h next month
i the month after next
j last August
k a week tomorrow
l the day before yesterday
m a week on Friday

6 (*possible answers*)
a Do you know any factories that can supply the components?
b Who can we approach to help with this project?
c Can you give me some recommendations?
d What are your logistics people like?
e How can I make myself known to those designers?
f Can we arrange a meeting to go through everything?

UNIT 3 Out of the office

1

MESSAGE

MESSAGE TO: John Beale
TIME: DATE:
FROM: Martin Biffen
PHONE No: 049-339-467-2938 (office number)
MOBILE No:
MESSAGE: Martin Biffen can't make lunch on Thursday. Please can you call him.

2 **a** He is at lunch.
It's 12 o'clock.
Please call him back.
b His visit to Madrid next week.
He asks Viktor to send him a message.
Two hours.

3 **a** iii **b** v
c viii **d** vi
e ii **f** vii
g i **h** iv

4 (*possible answers*)
a Let's postpone the meeting until next week.
b Please don't open the window.
c Shall we have lunch out a week on Monday?
d Perhaps you could call the HR department for me.
e Why don't I ask him to give you a ring?
f Would you mind not telling him I called?
g Shall I ask her to call you in the morning?
h Let me get you a coffee.

5 **a** off **b** down
c in; with **d** on
e with **f** to
g in **h** in / with
i for

UNIT 4 Introducing your company

1 **a** **i** is a practice of architects, engineers and
ii currently 200 people in it
iii is around 12 million pounds a year
iv is in London, but we also have overseas offices in Paris
v in the UK
b **i** The main company activity
ii the parent company employs something like 50,000 people
iii we have two manufacturing plants

2 acquisitions 9 business 3
clients 2 employees 5
profit 4 sale 7
subsidiaries 8 supplier 1
turnover 6

3 **a** eight point five one million square kilometres
b a (one) hundred and eighty-six point two million

c thirty-nine point five three million
d one point one four million square kilometres
e twenty seven point nine million
f fifteen point nine million
g two point seven eight million square kilometres
h forty-two point nine million

4 (*possible answers*)
a What type of company is it?
It's a private, family owned company.
b What are its main activities?
It manufactures electrical switches.
c Where are its main markets?
In California, and also in Kansas.
d How is the company organised?
There are three divisions: sales, production and administration.
e What is the job title of your boss?
His title is Area Sales Manager.
f Who does he/she report to?
He/She reports to the Vice-President, Sales.
g How many employees does the company have?
Forty-three full time, and others part time.
h Where is the company based?
The headquarters are in San Francisco.

5 **a** to **b** at
c to / for **d** in
e on **f** in
g from **h** to / for
i on **j** by

UNIT 5 Company profiles

1 Speaker 1 Speaker 2
a i **d** i
b ii **e** ii
c iii

2 **a** approximately four hectares
b from the city centre
c a freehold site
d approximately 30 years
e approximately £7 million and the budget for this year shows a budget of £$7^{1}/_{2}$ million
f the items which we manufacture for other people
g our own brand name
h export business
i all classes of
j secondary schools, higher education, to universities.

3 **a** as **b** state-owned
c monopoly **d** shares
e market **f** law
g competition **h** exclusive
i public **j** like
k general **l** shareholders
m majority **n** government

4 **a** do **b** doing
c make **d** do
e made **f** do
g make **h** making
i makes **j** make
k done / been doing

5 **a** am still working
b own/owns
c invest/are investing
d don't think
e takes up / is taking up
f go
g usually fly
h are doing/is doing

UNIT 6 Competitors

1 **a** **i** 3 **b** **i** 2
ii 2 **ii** 3
iii 1 **iii** 1

2 **a** iv **b** i
c ii **d** iv

3 (*possible answers*)
a What is your opinion of this month's sales results?
b Do you agree with your colleague about this?
c What's your view on/about the product?
d Does the project leader consider this (to be) a good investment?
e Who do the management think will replace the chairperson at Kazoloo?
f In your opinion is the product of/a good enough quality?
g Why do you think Brazil is such a good market for these components?

4 (*possible answers*)
a Our largest competitor is ten or twelve times bigger than us, but they are not our most dangerous competitor; they are the least important to us.
b What worries us most is the smaller companies, who are more flexible and quicker to react.
c The most important thing now is to be flexible. The faster your reaction is, the happier your customers are.

5 **a** profitable **b** specialists
c competition **d** producers
e investment **f** products
g competitors **h** production

UNIT 7 Your personal background

1 **Speaker 1**
a From Poitiers, in western France.
b For 23 years.
c Some are primary school age, and some are older than 18.
Speaker 2
d From Senegal.
e She's not working at the moment.
f One is a girl and three are boys.
Speaker 3
g She was born in Alloa, in Scotland.
h She has a daughter, 14, and a son, 12.

2

In the last month	has the speaker:
watched TV?	✓
read a book?	✓
done any gardening?	✗
had friends round for a meal?	✗
been to a restaurant?	✓
done any DIY (do-it-yourself)?	✓
been to exercise classes?	✗
been to the cinema?	✗
been to a nightclub?	✗
been to a sports club?	✓
been away on holiday?	✗
been to the theatre?	✗
been to the zoo?	✗
other	✓

3 **a** have to
b – haven't (have not)
– have
c had to **d** have; had
e hasn't (has not) **f** have; had to
g had to **h** have; had to

4 (*possible answers*)
a Accommodation: house, flat, tower block, bungalow, apartment
b Health: headache, bad back, broken arm, measles, toothache, asthma
c Interests: watching films, skiing, gardening, needlework, playing tennis, reading
d Occupation: secretary; managing, director, finance controller, project leader, clerical worker

5 **a** still **b** still
c yet **d** still
e again **f** still
g yet **h** still

6
a I i am born / ii was born in the south of Spain.
b How long i are you / ii have you been self-employed?
c i Did you / ii Have you ever had to fire someone?
d How i are your family? / ii have your family been?
e i Do you still work / ii Are you still working for the government?
f He doesn't agree with the new policies, so he i is resigned. / ii has resigned.
g I i am / ii have been in Sales all my life.
h The situation i hasn't changed / ii didn't change much since yesterday.

UNIT 8 Conditions of work

1 computer: speaker 3
desk: speaker 2
elevator/lift: speaker 4
shelf: speaker 5
seat: speaker 1

2 a were working b were getting
c were leaving d were working
e was trying f had been
g had made h had not received
i had happened
j had already spent
k had done / were doing
l had not done / were not doing
m were rising / had risen
n were falling / had fallen
o was looking
p were working

3 a What special benefits do you receive?
b Does your company pay your phone bills?
c Is the lighting bright enough for you to read?
d There were not enough workstations for everyone to use.
e The shelves were too high for me to reach.
f There were too many things for me to remember.

4 (*possible answers*)
Category 1: keyboard, hard drive, mouse, printer, scanner, screen
Category 2: cable, fuse, plug, socket, switch
Category 3: carpet, filing cabinet, desk, seat, shelves, shredder
Category 4: elevator, corridor, entrance, lift, stairs
Category 5: fan, air conditioning, radiator, lamp, spotlight

5 a scrutinising b dictating
c compose d fixing
e let f correct
g use h secure
i guarantee j find
k provide l recruit
m waste

UNIT 9 Job descriptions

1 a **An American administrative assistant**
Qualifications: A BA in Liberal Arts, Diploma in International Relations
Previous employment: Personnel
Current occupation: Office of the director of administration
b **An English production director**
Qualifications: Higher National Diploma in production engineering, a diploma in German (?)
Previous employment: Planning engineer
Current occupation: Project management
c **A Norwegian translator**
Qualifications: None mentioned
Previous employment: Secretary-translator
Current occupation: Currently not working

2 a = Person 3
b = Person 4
c = Person 1
d = Person 2

3 a – b with
c as; at d in
e –; at f with/in
g in h for; as

4 (*possible answers*)
a accountant executive – advertising
b steward – airlines
c chief cashier – banking
d systems analyst – computers
e cook – hotel / restaurant
f drug representative – pharmaceuticals
g estate agent – property
h machinist – textiles
i surveyor – civil engineering
j loss adjuster – insurance
k quality controller – car industry
l book-keeper – accountancy
m editor – publishing
n pit manager – mining
o shop assistant – retail trade
p ticket inspector – railways
Notes: drug representative = salesperson for a pharmaceutical company; machinist = person who works a machine;
pit manager = manager of a coal mine/pit

5 (*possible answers*)
a Yes, he did. b No, I don't.
c No, she isn't. d Yes, it must.
e No, it wasn't. f Yes, they would.
g No, it hasn't. h No, they hadn't.

6 a He's an interpreter and translator specialising in advertising, commerce, media, transport and legal fields.
b English
c He studied French and German, followed by a course in interpreting and translating.
d For Shell International and the UN.
e It's 40% interpreting, and 60% translating.
f He returns to the hotel to read paperwork for the next day.

UNIT 10 Buying products

1 a i used to use; ii always use
b iii had to use; iv used
c v used to use; vi used to; vii use
d viii used

2 a twenty-three slash oh nine eight seven six dash two two one B (23/09876-221B)
b twenty cubic metres ($20m^3$)

- **c** two, eleven, zero eight (2 11 08)
- **d** ninety-eight degrees centigrade (98°C)
- **e** thirteen thousand, two hundred and fifty (13,250)
- **f** twelve million, five hundred thousand pounds (£12,500,000)
- **g** Sixty-six per cent; two-thirds (66%; $^2/_3$)
- **h** Three-eighths; thirty-seven point five per cent ($^3/_8$; 37.5%)
- **i** ten metres by six point five metres (10×6.5)

3 **a** highly recommended
- **b** long lasting
- **c** extremely attractive; well made
- **d** very widely used
- **e** highly competitive
- **f** specially selected
- **g** beautifully designed
- **h** really well produced

4 **a** order **b** reference
- **c** plastic **d** stainless
- **e** out of stock **f** supply
- **g** delivery **h** in stock
- **i** manufacturers **j** discontinued
- **k** line **l** stock

5 (*possible answers*)
- **a** glass: hard, brittle, rigid, etc.
- **b** paper: soft, flexible, light, flammable
- **c** iron: hard, strong, rigid, heavy
- **d** PVC: tough, strong, flexible, man-made
- **e** copper: soft, flexible
- **f** gold: soft, heavy
- **g** wood: hard, tough, flammable
- **h** leather: soft, tough, strong
- **i** cotton: soft, flexible, flammable
- **j** nylon: soft, flexible, flammable, man-made
- **k** beef: tough, edible

6 **a** desk calculator with built-in transmitter
- **b** portable calculator transmitter
- **c** pen transmitter
- **d** telephone transmitter
- **e** plug adapter room transmitter
- **f** power socket transmitter
- **g** briefcase with built-in recording equipment

UNIT 11 Product descriptions

1 **a** Manufacturing
- **i** Individual components are welded together. (2)
- **ii** The truck is assembled and goes through final testing. (3)
- **iii** Steel plate is cut into shapes. (1)

b Fast-food catering
- **i** Then it's served across the counter. (3)
- **ii** We dispense accurate measures of mustard and ketchup. (2)
- **iii** We put the sesame seed bun in the toaster. (1)

2 a badminton racket – description c
a coat hanger – description e
a chess board – description d
an American football – description a
a golf club – description b

3 (*possible answers*)
- **a** have never seen
- **b** has he been working
- **c** have been working
- **d** have not noticed; has been happening
- **e** has the company hired
- **f** have lost; have done
- **g** have not stopped
- **h** have they decided

4 **a** How much does it cost?
- **b** Is this model suitable for my needs?
- **c** How often do they need servicing?
- **d** How long have they been producing this line?
- **e** Why did they change the specifications?
- **f** Have you got enough in stock?
- **g** When can you can deliver?
- **h** Is there a discount for quantity?

5 **a** The crystals are made by freezing the liquid.
- **b** The mixture is kept in the tank.
- **c** It is frozen to −5°C.
- **d** The temperature is constantly monitored.
- **e** It is left there for two hours.
- **f** Samples are taken for analysis.
- **g** The smallest crystals are chosen.
- **h** The larger ones are thrown away.

UNIT 12 Faults and breakdowns

1 **a** True **b** True
- **c** False **d** True
- **e** True **f** True

2 **a** faulty plastic smoke alarm
- **b** large South African mining company
- **c** new fibreglass tennis racquet
- **d** white ceramic reading lamp
- **e** adjustable liquid crystal display
- **f** cheap imported foreign goods
- **g** defective hydraulic component
- **h** new electronic security system

3 **a** down **b** with
- **c** out **d** out
- **e** in **f** with; out
- **g** to; about **h** for

4 **a** where / in which
- **b** – / that / which **c** whose
- **d** who / that **e** whose
- **f** which **g** – / which / that
- **h** which

UNIT 13 The services you provide and use

1 **a** purchasing **b** fleet
- **c** buy **d** outright
- **e** lease **f** expenses
- **g** per **h** company
- **i** repairs **j** in-house
- **k** tax **l** leasing
- **m** claim **n** expense

2 **a** True **b** True
- **c** False
  The speaker doesn't do anything that involves heights.
- **d** False
  The au pair does a little housework as well.
- **e** True

3 (*possible answers*)
- **a** We need to have/get the boilers serviced.
- **b** I have had/got the contracts signed.
- **c** Are you having/getting everything sorted out?
- **d** We need to have/get the whole factory demolished and rebuilt.
- **e** We sometimes had/got some market analysis done.
- **f** Shall I have/get some coffee brought in?
- **g** We didn't have/get a formal agreement prepared.
- **h** We had/got some photographs taken of the building.

4 (*possible answers*)
- **a** How much should we pay them?
- **b** Why must we change our suppliers?
- **c** Do we have to pay the rental quarterly?
- **d** How often does the machine need servicing?
- **e** What ought the service contract to include?
- **f** Where should I send the bill?
- **g** When ought the engineer to be here?
- **h** How much do we need to pay per month?

5 **a** ourselves **b** himself
c our own **d** my own
e yourselves **f** itself
g her own **h** myself

UNIT 14 Service issues

1 **a** a bank: Speaker 3
b an electrical service company: Speaker 1
c a hotel: Speaker 5
d a components supplier: Speaker 4
e an international courier: Speaker 2

2 **A: iii** I'd like to speak to Mr Diaz, please.
B: f Diaz speaking.
A: v Hello. This is Aminex here. It's about your account.
B: h What seems to be the problem?
A: vii It seems we haven't received your July payment yet.
B: e No, that's right, you haven't.
A: vi The terms of our agreement are payment not later than the third of the month.
B: a Yes. I know that.
A: ii Then can we expect your payment today?
B: b No, I'm afraid we're not paying this bill.
A: viii Could you explain that, please?
B: g Your last delivery was very poor quality.
A: i I'm sorry to hear that.
B: d I told Mr Sanchez. I said we were withholding payment until it was sorted out.
A: iv I didn't know that. I'll talk to Mr Sanchez.
B: c He'll tell you all about it!

3 *(possible answers)*
a We've had to cancel the course due to insufficient demand.
b The plane was diverted because of fog in Lima.
c We have cancelled the deal on account of problems with our suppliers.
d All flights are delayed due to bad weather.
e We have changed our proposal as a result of new government regulations.
f Business has been good on account of the hot weather.
g We have had to recall that batch as a result of customer complaints.
h They have stopped making this line due to insufficient demand.

4 **a** must have been
b should have arrived
c should have/could have let
d should have asked
e must have sent
f could have/should have sent
g could have/should have made
h must have caused

UNIT 15 Service industries

1

	Speaker 1	Speaker 2	Speaker 3
an hourly rate		✓	
fee		✓	✓
expenses		✓	
a commission	✓		

2 **a** **i** 250 contracts in the north-west
ii 1,900 people
b **iii** major employers in the area
iv for two to three thousand staff.
c **v** training programme in food hygiene and safety
vi their knowledge of nutrition and safety regulations

3 **a** in; for **b** in
c by **d** to
e in **f** for
g for **h** for

4 *(possible answers)*
a We specialise in the interior design of offices.
b Our clients range in size from small to very large.
c We have some very large clients, such as IBM and HP.
d They offer a complete service from design consultancy to supplying plants and flowers.
e We employ 100 staff, both full time and part time.
f We charge extra fees for interior decoration and design.
g Customers who are on contracts are charged monthly.
h We feel we offer an important service to our clients.

5 **a** fee **b** quote
c commission **d** charges
e commission **f** charges
g discount **h** price, charge

6 *(possible answers)*
a They can't have meant that. They must have meant 2,000.
b You must have misunderstood. They probably said $300 thousand.
c S/he can't have said 'fired'; s/he must have meant 'hired'.
d She can't have said that. She must have made a mistake.

UNIT 16 Looking after visitors

1 **a** iii **b** i **c** ii

2 To check who is speaking and to fill in the gaps, follow the audioscript for this exercise on pages 133–134 of this book.

3 **a** Where do you usually take your foreign clients?
b Do you ever take them on a river boat trip?
c We almost never take customers to sports events.
d We don't often go to the opera.
e They nearly always meet at the airport.
f We go out if there's time, but more frequently we just go to the canteen.
g I have occasionally travelled by boat.
h We hardly ever take clients to a club.

4 *(possible answers)*
a **A:** He was going to buy tickets for the opera.
B: But she said she would prefer to go to the cinema.
b **A:** I was going to invite you to dinner tonight.
Or perhaps you would prefer to come tomorrow?
c **A:** Were you planning to do anything tonight?
B: No. I would prefer to go to bed.
d **A:** We were thinking of visiting Australia.
B: But our daughter would rather go to Peru.
e **A:** Were you planning to send them a 'thank you' letter?
B: No. I would rather phone them.
f **A:** We were thinking of walking into the town centre.
B: Wouldn't you prefer to go by car?

5 **a** 2 **b** 3
c 1 **d** 3
e 2 **f** 1
g 3 **h** 2
i 3

UNIT 17 Hotels and restaurants

1 Exchange 1: k Exchange 2: o
Exchange 3: l Exchange 4: p

Exchange 5: c Exchange 6: n
Exchange 7: g Exchange 8: e
Exchange 9: m Exchange 10: d
Exchange 11: j Exchange 12: b
Exchange 13: a Exchange 14: f
Exchange 15: h Exchange 16: i

2 (*possible answers*)
- **a** Can you book me a room with a balcony.
- **b** The bar will be closed tomorrow.
- **c** Could you prepare our bill, please?
- **d** Do you have the name of the French restaurant the doorman recommended?
- **e** We'd like a table for four.
- **f** I left my umbrella in the restaurant last night.
- **g** Don't wait for me.
- **h** How are you going to get home?

3 **a** say **b** says
c talk **d** talk
e says **f** talked (or spoke)
g said **h** tell
i says **j** speak
k say **l** say

4

meat	seafood	vegetable	fruit	drink
beef	cod	asparagus	apple	cocoa
chicken	herring	broccoli	banana	coffee
ham	lobster	cabbage	grapefruit	lager
lamb	prawn	carrot	lemon	lemonade
mutton	salmon	mushroom	melon	rum
pork	sole	potato	orange	tea
sausage	trout		strawberry	water
	tuna		tomato	

Some examples of things you can make from these foods:
tomato soup, beef stew,
pickled herring, pork casserole,
strawberry shortcake, potato pancakes,
mushroom risotto.

5 A typical British place setting

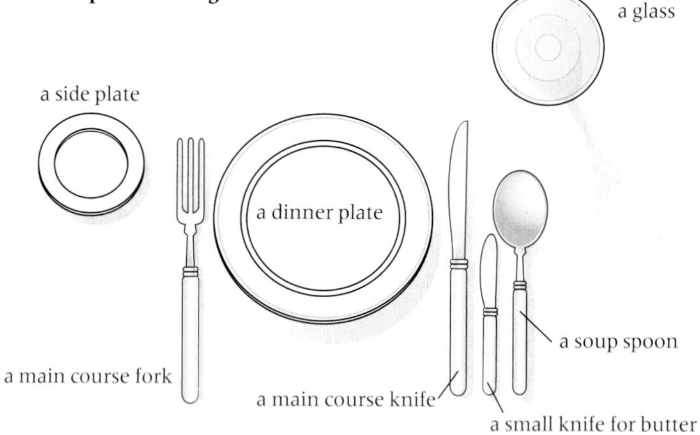

UNIT 18 Corporate entertaining

1 **a** v **b** iii, vii
c i **d** viii, ii
e vi, iv

2 **a** motor racing **b** swimming
c rugby **d** skiing

3

Adjective	Adverb	Comparative adverb
automatic	automatically	more automatically
early	early	earlier
extreme	extremely	–
good	well	better
late	late	later
long	long	longer
quick	quickly	more quickly
realistic	realistically	more realistically
slow	slowly	more slowly
smooth	smoothly	more smoothly

(*possible answers*)
a earlier **b** smoothly
c later **d** automatically
e more quickly (quicker) **f** long
g extremely **h** more slowly

4 (*possible answers*)
- **a** We could see if they are free in the evening, instead.
- **b** I think you might be able to contact him on his mobile.
- **c** I'd recommend a sports event – perhaps a local football match.
- **d** Why not have a buffet-style meal instead?
- **e** Have you thought about contacting an events planner for advice?
- **f** How about doing it right away?

5
- **a** any tickets left
- **b** a group of five
- **c** entrance tickets
- **d** includes transportation
- **e** to the main events
- **f** no parking
- **g** every eight minutes
- **h** the standard package
- **i** the booking

UNIT 19 Setting up meetings

1

	Annual General Meeting	Export managers' meetings	Team meetings	Monthly meetings	Working groups	Formal meetings	Meetings with an agenda
A French union representative				✓	✓		✓
A New Zealand director of a real estate company	✓			✓		✓	✓
An Irish export manager		✓	✓	✓		✓	✓

2 **a** at **b** –
c by **d** for
e in **f** at; in
g to/till **h** for; –
i by; at

3 **a** at this end **b** looks as if
c to be able **d** in time
e as though the room
f has been put off **g** it's been moved
h be able to make **i** hear from you

4 **a** vi **b** iv
c ii; v; ix **d** viii
e vii **f** i
g ii; v; ix **h** iii
i ii; v; ix

(*possible examples*)
Someone had better take notes.
If there's going to be a rail strike, we'd better call off the sales meeting.
I don't know where their office is, so we'd better meet up in the hotel lobby.
We'd better not change the time; it'll confuse everyone.
I'd better read through the agenda.
If you want to question the people running the company, you'd better attend the AGM.
I can't make the meeting. I'd better send my apologies.
We'd better not put the board meeting off; people will think something is wrong.

5 **a** We should be able to get through all the points.
b We won't be able to start till after lunch.
c Sorry, I wasn't able to come to the last meeting.
d I enjoy being able to drive when I want.
e It's hard to get a job without being able to work.
f We all have to be able to operate the machines.
g She must be able to speak some English.
h Several people will be able to attend the meeting.

UNIT 20 Meeting procedures

1 **a** A Russian civil servant: disagrees because English is widely used.
b An American administrative assistant: disagrees because it would cause tremendous difficulties to replace English.
c A French union representative: agrees because English is putting a lot of people at a disadvantage.
d An English production manager: disagrees because so many systems are using English.
e A Scottish accountant: disagrees because English is the most commonly used language.

2 **a** hoping **b** Joseph Stalin
c corporate **d** everyone
e Parkinson

3 **a** i, iv **b** iv
c iii **d** i
e ii **f** ii, iv
g iii, iv **h** i
i i, iii, iv **j** ii, iii, iv
k iv **l** i, iii, iv
m iii, iv **n** ii, iv

4 (*possible answers*)
a If they didn't smoke most smokers would support the ban.
b Would you be able to make it if we arranged the meeting for tomorrow?
c If we were to pay more, we'd get better quality.
d I should/would check the facts, if I were you.
e The speaker would prefer it if you didn't ask questions until the end.
f What would you do if you were in my position?
g Would it be better if we started after lunch?
h If I didn't have to go to this meeting, I would do it myself.

5 (*possible answers*)
a iii **b** iv
c v **d** i
e ii

UNIT 21
Meeting follow-up

1

	preparation	clear agenda	sticking to the agenda	specific time limit	restricted numbers	clear objectives	clear lead from the chair	willingness to compromise	willingness to share ideas	good minutes
An American marine pollution engineer		✓		✓						
A French union representative	✓					✓	✓			
A Dutch customer services manager		✓	✓		✓		✓			✓

2 **a** to send **b** chair
c to meet
d to circulate, or to type up
e inform **f** to cover
g to visit **h** to be
i have
j to circulate, or to type up

3 (*possible answers*)
a 'I think that Julio should chair the meeting.'
b 'Why don't you circulate the agenda in advance?'
c 'If I were you, I wouldn't reply.'
d 'Don't accept less than 50 cents a unit.'
e 'It's not a good idea to be late.'
f 'Could you report back at the next meeting?'
g 'Do you think we should change our supplier?'
h 'Would you mind taking the minutes?'

4 (*possible answers*)
a ix Were you at yesterday's meeting?
b vi How did the meeting go?
c v Did you manage to get through everything on the agenda?
d ii Did the meeting overrun?
e iv Who chaired the meeting?
f i Did anyone take the minutes?
g vii Are they going to circulate the minutes?
h iii When is the next meeting?
i viii Were you able to contact the contractor?

5 **a** attached **b** technical
c Engineering **d** through
e document **f** comments
g back **h** regards

UNIT 22 Arranging a visit

1 (*possible answers*)
a Go straight through Rostock, till you get to the bridge. Then left after the bridge into the Strand. The office is halfway down, a big, red-stone building.
b Take Route 1, the Glen Highway, for 200 miles. Take the only right turn. Travel 115 miles to Valdez. Turn left at the Shell station.
c From the Termini station, take Linea B to Circo Massimo, the third station. When you come out of the station, the building is on the right.
d Take the bus from Arlanda to central Stockholm; it stops at the station. Take the underground to Mariavik, the blue line. About an hour from the airport to her office.

2 (*possible answers*)
18.20, arr Kuala Lumpur;
Flight AL 308
By car to Hotel Intercontinental
20.30, dinner with local reps
June 7 09.00, meet Linda Thian, KRT Engineering
11.15, visit to Palford Ltd
13.00, lunch at hotel with lawyers
14.45, car pick up at hotel
16.35, dep Sydney, flight AL216
a – Will he be staying at the Hilton?
– No, he'll be staying at Intercontinental.
b – How will he be travelling to the hotel?
– By car.
c – What will he be doing at 21.00 on the 6th?
– He will be having dinner with the local reps.
d – Will he be visiting Palford Ltd?
– Yes, he will, at 11.15 on the 7th.
e – What time will he be leaving the hotel for the airport?
– At 14.45.
f – How long will he be staying in Malaysia?
– Only a couple of days.
g – Is he free at 9am on the 7th?
– No, he'll be meeting Linda Thian, from KRT Engineering.

3 (*possible examples*)
a I hope to meet you while you are here.
b She will be in the States during July.
c She's going to be there for six days in all.
d She'll visit you while she is in Boston.
e You can contact her at the Farrington Inn during her stay.
f You can do some work during the journey.
g I won't see you for over a week.
h Will you have time to visit the pyramids while you are in Egypt?

4 **a** to **b** at **c** at
d at **e** to **f** to
g to **h** of **i** in
j in **k** to **l** from
m to

5 (*possible response*)

Dear ...
Thank you for your letter dated .... I was pleased to receive details of your schedule.
With regard to your request for advice, here are some tips.
- When attracting attention, we normally say 'Excuse me', especially to waiters/waitresses.
- We normally tip taxi drivers and waiters/waitresses, but not bar staff. Ten per cent is about right.
- When waiting, we usually form a queue.
- It is not necessary to shake hands every time you meet people.

Please contact me if you need further help.
I look forward to seeing you.
Best regards

UNIT 23 Abroad on business

1 **Pros**
Seeing new places: Speaker 3
You can concentrate 100%: Speaker 1
Tasting strange foods: Speaker 3
Meeting new people: Speaker 3
The pleasure/enjoyment of travel: Speaker 2
Cons
Long-haul flights: Speaker 3
No back-up/support: Speaker 2
Using another language: Speaker 1
Being by yourself in hotels: Speaker 3
It's tiring/stressful: Speakers 1, 2
Not knowing where things are: Speaker 2

2 **a** Arriving at a hotel: 4
b At the hotel reception: 5
c Checking train times: 8
d In a taxi: 1
e At an airport information desk: 7
f Hiring a car: 6
g At a service station: 2
h Missing luggage: 3

3 (*possible answers*)
a Where will you be staying while you are here?
b I'll take a pill as soon as I get on the plane.
c When I reach New York, I will go to bed for an hour or two.
d I won't sleep till I get to Berlin.
e Will you see John before he leaves?
f While we are at the conference, we will not have much time.
g As soon as they get here, I will give you a call.
h Will you check the details with me before you book the flight?

4 (*possible answers*)
a I find it difficult to sleep on planes.
b Some people find it easy to cope with jet lag.
c We are meeting in Paris rather than Rome.
d I usually go by train rather than fly.
e It is impossible to see where we are.
f It is not necessary to reserve a seat.
g Book a four star hotel, rather than a five star.
h It is important to complete the job as soon as possible.

5 **a** The call was interrupted.
b The weekend before leaving Montreal, or perhaps for a day during the conference.
c He suggests that Allen flies from Montreal, spends the evening with them, then visits the plant the next day.
d Yes, he will.
e Not yet. She will when it's been confirmed.
f Nothing. It's free time.

UNIT 24 Returning from a business trip

1 (*sample notes*)
Speaker 1: It was short trip to Almaty and Astana. The purpose was to talk to distributors, and to plan promotion. It was part business and part social.

Speaker 2: A two-day trip to Paris. She had lunch with potential users. It went very well.

Speaker 3: A trip to Istanbul, to present a design to a bank. They haven't got the job yet.

2 **a** Organisation of Petroleum Exporting Countries (OPEC)
b World Health Organization (WHO)
c International Monetary Fund (IMF)
d North American Free Trade Agreement (NAFTA)
e Association of South East Asian Nations (ASEAN)

3 **a** in case **b** if **c** so that
d if **e** if **f** so that
g in case **h** so that **i** in case

4 (*possible answers*)
a How far is it to Sao Paulo?
b How long does it take to get there?
c Does it take that long by plane?
d What were you doing there?
e How long were you there?
f What was your hotel like?
g Where exactly was it?
h What does BMES stand for?

UNIT 25 Personal finances

1 **a** False **b** False
c True **d** False

Why the speaker recommends a visit to Iceland

- The food is excellent.
- If you're coming from the UK, the pound is strong against the krona, so hotels and so on are cheaper than they have been in the past.
- It's a great place if you like fishing.
- There's some fantastic scenery.

2 **a** 4,000 **b** 4,000 **c** 4,000
d 2,000 **e** 4,000 **f** 8,000

3 **a** on; to **b** on **c** as; as
d on/in **e** for **f** on
g by **h** in

4 **a** sign **b** take care **c** leave
d check **e** write down **f** expires
g stolen

5 (*possible order*)
A: What's wrong?
B: My house was broken into yesterday.
A: Did they take much?
B: They took a computer and some other items.
A: Were they worth a lot?
B: They were worth about $800.
A: Are you insured?
B: Yes, I'm going to make a claim.
A: What's the name of your insurance company?
B: I can't remember. I'll have to check.

Examples of expanded phrases

- I'm sorry to hear that you were broken into yesterday.
- But I thought you had an alarm system fitted to your house.
- I know the feeling; we were burgled last year.

6 (*possible answers*)
a He did. I remember him doing it.
b I do spend money on hobbies, but not so much on other things.
c She does. I've seen her do it.
d He did do it. I was there.
e You do know her. You met at my house.
f I do like your new car.

UNIT 26 Company finances

1 **a** i **b** iii **c** ii

2 **Speaker 1**
Overall performance: good
Comments: difficult trading conditions, especially in food and drink sector
Trading profit: £1009 million
% change: up 12.3%

Speaker 2
Overall performance: very successful
Comments: another successful year, with profits and sales both up
Trading profit: $362 million
% change: up 6%

Speaker 3
Overall performance: disappointing
Comments: lower-than-expected sales
Trading profit: £32.4 million
% change: down 3%

3 **a** The shareholders approved the accounts at the AGM.
b The management has set tough targets for the coming year.
c We expect turnover to rise again this year.
d We achieved this by offering value for money.
e Our customers owe us a lot of money.
f We should always plough back profits.
g We must transfer the funds soon.
h The market values the company at between 30 and 40 million dollars.

4 (*possible answers*)
Interest rates have fallen this year.
Our fixed assets are worth €8 million.
The balance sheet looks very healthy.
We receive dividend payments twice a year.
It was a very impressive financial report.
High productivity is a key factor in our success.
We have worked out a new pricing formula.
What is your total revenue for the year?
We have set ourselves high productivity targets.

5 **a** debtor **b** employee
c revenue **d** assets
e profit **f** gross
g lend

6 **Organisations:** NATO North Atlantic Treaty Organisation), EU (European Union), ASEAN (Association of South East Asian Nations), ALADI (Latin American Integration Association)
Job titles: CEO (chief executive officer), PA (personal assistant), MD (managing director)
Company departments: IT (Information Technology), PR (Public Relations)
Correspondence/documents: re (regarding, in connection with), PTO (please turn over), cc (copies to), encl/enc (enclosed), NB (note; take special note that), pp (on behalf of), ref. (reference; with reference to), att/attn (for the attention of)
Others: AGM (annual general meeting), EGM (extraordinary general meeting), Inc (incorporated), VIP (very important person), RPI (retail price index), PCL/plc (public limited company), bal (balance), i.e. (that is; in other words)

UNIT 27 Payment issues

1 **a** 12–1300 **b** $^3/_4$
c $100m^2$ **d** 352 ÷ 2.7
e 99.9% **f** $37.50 × 36
g $5^1/_2m^3$ **h** 2.06m – 1.73m
i 15.99 **j** 136/D

2 **a** We'll start supplying you again providing/provided we receive payment within seven days.
b Providing/provided you let us have the order number, we will pay you.

c Providing/provided we receive an order reference, we can supply the goods immediately.
d Unless you are planning to export the goods, I am afraid you will have to pay the sales tax.
e You can borrow my pen providing/provided you let me have it back.
f Providing/provided you send it today, it'll be here in time.
g Unless you send it today, I won't have time to look at it.
h Unless we sort out the problem immediately, we will lose the contract.

3 (*possible answers*)
a Apparently there has been a query on this.
b It seems that payment was passed last week.
c We don't appear to have received it.
d You seem to have paid twice.
e It appears they sent the payment last week.
f Apparently, they have paid by cheque.
g Apparently the invoice details don't appear to tally with our records.
h They don't appear to have got our letter.

4 a each/every b each
c each d every
e each/every f each
g each/every h each/every

5 a invoice b outstanding
c guarantee d expand
e overdue f ludicrous

UNIT 28 Preparing for a presentation

1 **Speaker 1**
✓ the type/size of room
✓ think through the presentation beforehand
✓ check technical equipment
Speaker 2
✓ the type/size of room
✓ seating arrangements
✓ run through the presentation beforehand

2 (*possible order*)
A: We'll begin in five minutes' time if you're ready.
B: Fine.
A: How are you feeling? Would you like a glass of water?
B: No, no. I'm fine, thanks.
A: Are you used to doing this?
B: I'm getting used to it.
A: Good. Is there anything else you need?
B: How do you adjust the projector?
A: On the side, here.
B: Perhaps it should move further from the screen.
A: Yes, but the lead isn't long enough.
B: Could you get hold of an extension lead?
A: Yes, sure. We've got one here somewhere.

3 a on b – c for
d – e – f to
g at h by

4 a We're used to not having a canteen on site.
b The company never used to employ students.
c I'm used to working abroad.
d We used to have a training department.
e I'll have to get used to doing it.
f I'm not used to giving long presentations.
g The shareholders always used to get a report.
h I can't get used to chairing the committee.

5 (*suggested answers*)
a iii b v c i
d v e i f ii
g iv h i

UNIT 29 Presenting facts and figures

1

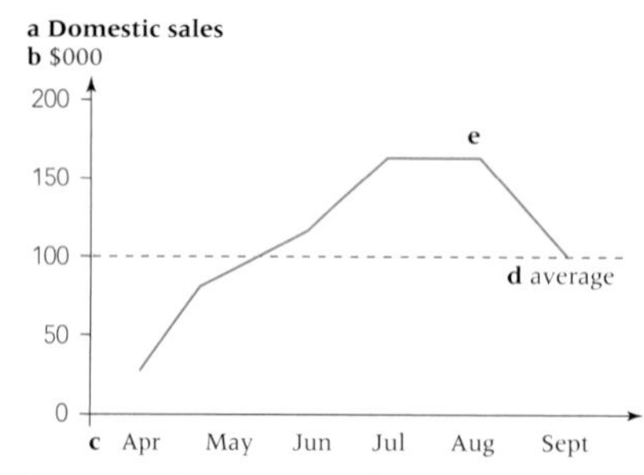

2 a making b to send
c saying d to do/doing
e working/work f to work
g to mention h work

Notes
e.g. prices started to rise/rising – there is no change in meaning.
a We stopped making them = We didn't make them any more.
We stopped to make them = We stopped something else to make them.
b I remembered to send = I didn't forget.
I remember sending = I can recall the event.
c I don't remember saying = I don't recall the event.
I didn't remember to say = I forgot to say it.
d They don't like doing/to do – there is no change in meaning.
e I watched them work/working – there is no significant change in meaning.
f They want to work – the *-ing* form is not possible here.
g The *-ing* form is not possible here.
h make them work – work is the only possibility here.

3 a between b In c over
d on e on f for

4 (*possible answers*)
a The overall rate was just under 9%.
b Sales average £4,500 per hour.
c On average, we make a sale every five seconds.
d We sell twice as much as we did four years ago.
e We employ half the number of staff we did two years ago.
f Only one in three of our products are sold through supermarkets.
g These figures represent our average sales per city.

UNIT 30 Delivering a presentation

1 i c ii a iii d iv b
v f vi e

2 1 d 2 b 3 f 4 a
5 e 6 c

3 1 c 2 b 3 a 4 c
5 a 6 b 7 b 8 a

4 (*possible answers*)
a 4 b 6 c 3 d 5
e 8 f 7 g 1 h 2

5 a in spite of b even though
c because d in case
e in spite of f due to
g in case h although

Audioscripts

UNIT 1 Everyday business contacts

1 **Authentic listening**

a **A Swedish financial controller**

Well, English is the official language of this organisation, so I use English on a daily basis, for instance, when I write reports, when I talk to my colleagues and also when I speak over the phone – which sometimes may cause a bit of a problem because on these occasions you don't see the person you talk to, and you don't get immediate response for what you're saying.

b **A Chilean clerk**

Well, we need English most of the time to read the documents that comes, and in order to check them with the books that we use, and addresses, and, you know, most of the work is done in English, Erm … I don't have much problem with spoken English. Whenever I have to write something, that might be some problem there.

Notes

Non-standard usage

Speaker a: 'the person you talk to'
(standard usage = the person you are talking to)
'response for'
(standard usage = response to)

Speaker b: 'the documents that comes'
(standard usage = the documents that come)
'that might be some problem'
(standard usage = there might be a problem)

2 **Short telephone conversations**

1 **A:** Hello. Is that Tarmo?
B: Speaking.
A: Hello, Tarmo. It's Teresa Milo here. Have you got a minute?
B: Hi Teresa. Yes, sure. Go ahead.
A: It's about Thursday's meeting. I need to …

2 **A:** Esther Briggs.
B: Esther. Hi! It's Maurice Penn here. Are you busy?
A: Yes, I'm in a meeting at the moment. Can I call you back this afternoon? About three o'clock your time?
B: Yes, of course. Speak to you later.

3 **A:** Is there anything else? Have we covered everything?
B: Just one thing. Could you ask Helmut to call me? Could you tell him I called?
A: Sure. I'll give him the message.

UNIT 2 Developing contacts

1 **Contacts abroad**

- So tell me something about the people you work with?
- Sure. Obviously I have a lot to do with the production people here in the factory and our agents abroad. Every day there are enquiries about orders. Are they ready? When will they be ready? Why aren't they ready? Etcetera. Occasionally a customer will call me direct, but usually queries go through our agents.
- How many agents do you have?
- I'm afraid I can't tell you how many there are worldwide, but in my area – which covers North Africa, Spain/Portugal – and Greece/Turkey, we have five. Our North African agent is based in Rabat in Morocco and we have agents in Madrid, Lisbon, Athens and Istanbul.
- And how are communications with these agents? Good?
- Pretty good on the whole. Although we are currently having some problems with our Lisbon agent. We appointed an English guy who lives in Lisbon, but he doesn't seem to know how to sell there. We're looking for someone else for that area.
- How do you find a new agent?
- Mainly through contacts.
- No language problems with your agents?
- No, they all speak good English. There are no problems.

UNIT 3 Out of the office

1 **Leaving a phone message**

- Yes, hello. Er. My name's Martin Biffen – that's B-I- double F-E-N – of Star Hotels. I'm trying to contact John Beale. I'm meeting him on Thursday for lunch, and I can't make it. That's John Beale – B-E-A-L-E – to say I can't meet him for lunch, on Thursday. Could he please call me? My office number is 049-339-467-2938.

2 **Trying to make contact**

a
- Can I speak to Pedro Ramez, please?
- I am afraid you just missed him. He is with some clients.
- What time is it in Spain?
- It's 12 o'clock. Mr Ramez should be back in his office at 12.30 our time. Where are you calling from? Can I take a message?
- I'm calling from Moscow, and, yes, could you tell Mr Ramez that Viktor Tomasov called and ask him to call me back. He's got my number.
- Yes, of course. I'll ask him to call you as soon as he gets back.

b
- Hello, is that Viktor?
- Speaking.
- Hello, Viktor. Pedro here. I hear that you called.
- Yes, that's right. I always seem to call you at a bad time. It's about my visit to Madrid next week. I'm afraid I won't know whether I can make it on Tuesday until tomorrow morning. Does it give you enough time to organise everything if I let you know at 10 o'clock my time?
- That's 8 o'clock in Spain. Yes, that would be fine. Send me a message and I'll speak to you later in the day.
- Thanks Pedro. Bye.

UNIT 4 Introducing your company

1 Authentic listening

a The Managing director of an architectural firm

Our company is a practice of architects, engineers and interior designers. It has currently 200 people in it, and was the first architectural practice to be quoted on the London Stock Exchange. We design buildings either as individual architects or engineers, or combined together to form a full multi-professional team. Our current turnover is around 12 million pounds a year. Our head office is in London, but we also have overseas offices in Paris, Berlin and Dubai. Our principal work is in the UK, but we're expanding …

b The Production director of a fork-lift manufacturer

The main company activity is to produce materials-handling equipment in the form of fork-lift trucks. Our company – is part of a larger group which is a German-based company which has interests not only in material handling but also in construction and plant, and production of technical gases. Throughout the world, the parent company employs something like 50,000 people. In the UK we have two manufacturing plants making fork-lift trucks – one concentrating on electric trucks and the other on engine-driven trucks. There are further manufacturing plants both in Germany and in France, also producing fork-lift trucks for the European market.

Note

Both speakers are English.

2 Company details

- What do you know about HSD?
- We're a supplier of theirs. They're one of our clients.
- They're in electricals, right?
- Yes, but that's not their main business. Most of the profit's in the construction side. Most of the employees, too.
- They did well last year. Good profits. Was that on a bigger turnover?
- Partly. It was also because of the sale of one of their subsidiaries in the States. That brought in quite a lot of money.
- Are they interested in making any acquisitions, do you know?
- I don't know but I could find out.

UNIT 5 Company profiles

1 Authentic listening

Speaker 1: An English merchant banker

The business is centred in London and it has two main operating units outside London – one based in Dublin and one based in Zurich. And I suppose the parts of the business fall into three separate, fairly distinct, categories, one of which is a securities-related business and involves the selling of large blocks of securities in the professional market. Another is an investment management business, which is a business which relies on attracting funds from individuals and also from large institutions, and managing them. And at the centre of the business is the traditional merchant bank, which has got two main activities, one of which is advisory and the other of which is financing.

Speaker 2: The English manager of a fast-food outlet

The basic structure of the company itself is a partnership: a licensee and a franchise. An individual can buy a part of the company and supply his public how he feels need to. In each country, there's a different licensee and a different franchising network. But there are support departments for each one of those: a head office, a training department, an accounts department. They're all here. But the company runs those. The manager himself actually runs his own business.

Notes

Speaker 1: the professional market = the market for institutional buyers, not the general public

Speaker 2: non-standard usage

'a licensee and a franchise'

(standard usage: a licensee and a franchisee)

'how he feels need to'

(standard usage: how he feels he needs to)

2 An overview of a stationery company

We are manufacturing stationers in Manchester, England. Our company employs 160 people and we operate on a site of approximately four hectares. We are approximately five miles from the city centre. The site which we operate from is a freehold site, and we have been here for approximately 30 years. Last year we had a turnover of approximately £7 million and the budget for this year shows a projected turnover of £7½ million. This turnover is split between the items which we manufacture for other people, and items which we manufacture under our own brand name. Our own brand products are sold to our customers via our own sales and marketing department and distributed in our own vehicles to our customers throughout the United Kingdom. We have a small amount of export business. Our products are primarily designed for use in educational situations, and our customers include all classes of education from primary schools through secondary schools, higher education, to universities.

Notes

- manufacturing stationer = a company which produces notepads, files, folders, etc.
- four hectares = approximately ten acres
- five miles = approximately eight kilometres

UNIT 6 Competitors

1 Authentic listening

a A production director

There is very intense competition in the materials-handling industry. I think our company has an advantage, based on many years' experience in the materials-handling field, and also the ability to introduce innovative solutions to particular problems. And this, combined with our very firmly established markets – specially within Europe – has helped us to maintain our market share in the face of competition from our competitors.

b A consulting engineer

Well, as a consulting engineer in the water industry, our market is really divided into two parts – that is, the home market and the overseas market. At home, we have very intense competition from a number of consulting engineering firms. The problem in the United Kingdom at the moment is that there are too many firms chasing too little work and consequently the whole market is dominated by price. If we move overseas, we find that our reputation is far more dominant in the way we get our work, and, for example, when we're competing for World Bank projects, it isn't the lowest price which gets the job.

2 Comparing companies

- We have two industrial plants. One in Switzerland and one in Chile.
- How do they compare in terms of costs?
- Well, Switzerland is an expensive country, and Chile is relatively cheap, so naturally it's more expensive to run a business of that sort in Switzerland.
- What about size?
- The Chilean plant is far bigger than the Swiss one. It's probably the biggest in South America.
- Does that make it more profitable?
- It's difficult to say. At the moment, when we compare them, profitability is about the same. There's not much difference. One problem is that the Chilean plant is relatively old. In some ways it needs to be modernised, whereas the Swiss plant is new.

UNIT 7 Your personal background

1 Authentic listening

Speaker 1
I'm originally from France – from the western part of France, from a town called Poitiers. I've been living in this country for 23 years. I have a house in the south-west of London, in Clapham. I have four children, some of whom still go to primary school and some of whom go to university.

Speaker 2
I'm from Senegal and I'm living in Camberwell with my wife and four kids. My wife is not working at the moment and the three boys are attending school in London. The small one is only living with her mum at home.

Speaker 3
I live in Basingstoke. I'm married. I have two children: a 14 year-old daughter and a 12 year-old son. I was born in a place called Alloa in Scotland, which is half-way between Glasgow and Edinburgh.

Notes
Speaker 2: Camberwell is in south London.
Non-standard usage: 'The small one is only living with her mum …' (standard usage: The small one is the only one living with her mum …)
Speaker 3: Basingstoke is a town in the south of England; the speaker has a Scottish accent.

2 Leisure interests

Let me run through your list. In the last month I have watched quite a lot of TV. I've been lazy. I read a good book last week, a novel by Dan Brown. It's been too cold to do any gardening. I've been unsociable and I've not had any friends round for ages, but we have had a few meals out. I've put up a couple of shelves – I suppose that counts for D-I-Y. I'm sorry to say that I've taken no exercise at all, and I haven't been anywhere. That answers a lot of the questions on your list. I never have time to go to the cinema. As for the others, I don't go to clubs or coffee bars and never go to the theatre. I last went to the zoo when I was ten years old. What about you?

UNIT 8 Conditions of work

1 In the office building

Speaker 1
This is what I use when I'm working. It revolves and the height is adjustable and so is the back.

Speaker 2
This is where I work. I don't have room for everything at the moment. I really need a bigger working surface.

Speaker 3
This is what I'm using at the moment. It's very light and the screen is detachable. It has a fantastic battery life. I like it because it fits very easily in my briefcase.

Speaker 4
I was working on the 2nd floor and had to go to the 7th. It wasn't working, so I had to use the stairs. When I got there I found I'd forgotten an important file and it still wasn't working.

Speaker 5
We need at least one more. We've got all these books and files, and we have to put them on the floor at the moment.

UNIT 9 Job descriptions

1 Authentic listening

a An American administrative assistant
I studied for four and a half years and I majored in Fine Arts and I came out with a BA – Bachelor of Arts in Liberal Arts. Thereafter I moved to the United Kingdom and I travelled for the first year and after a few years I studied international relations. I gained a diploma in international relations from the London School of Economics. I thereafter worked in (the) personnel section for about six years. Now I'm posted in the office of the director of administration.

b An English production director
I left college with a Higher National Diploma in production engineering and during that time that I was at college I was able to also spend some time working in Germany, which enabled me to leave college with a language qualification as well. I worked for a number of firms before finally coming to this company, where I started as a planning engineer, specifying manufacturing methods. I spent about ten years in this role before moving on to project management and becoming more involved with the introduction of new products into the manufacturing process.

c A Norwegian translator
I'm Norwegian. I was born in Oslo. I came to England 16 years ago to work for an aluminium company as a secretary–translator. I later went on to work in the City, for a British bank with Norwegian connections and, again, I did a lot of translating and secretarial work. Then I got married and I'm now planning to go back into paid employment as a translator.

2 Describing appearances and dress

a
- What does she look like?
- She's quite tall with straight, blonde hair. She's wearing a silk blouse and a knee-length black skirt.

b He's quite tall. He's wearing a dark suit and a tie. He's got short, curly hair.
c She's medium height, with dark, quite curly hair, and she's wearing a dark trouser-suit.
d He's got thinning dark hair, quite long. He's wearing a dark jacket and trousers and no tie.

UNIT 10 Buying products

1 *used to* and the verb *to use*

a I used to use the fax machine all the time, but now I use email. It's far more convenient.
b I had to use an old PC last week. I hadn't used one for ages.
c I can't think of any products which we used to use. All I can think of is people. We used to have a workforce of 32. Now we use two robots, and we have a workforce of six.
d We installed a wireless system and for the last few years we have used that.

2 Numbers and symbols

a The product reference number is twenty-three slash oh nine eight seven six dash two one B.
b We need about twenty cubic metres.
c The date I've got is two, eleven, zero eight.
d Water boils here at about ninety-eight degrees centigrade.
e The company employs thirteen thousand, two hundred and fifty people worldwide.
f We've spent twelve million, five hundred thousand pounds on development this year.
g Sixty-six per cent of the workforce are employed in this plant – that's two-thirds.
h Three-eighths – that's thirty-seven point five per cent – of company personnel are employed abroad.
i We need a space ten metres by six point five metres.

UNIT 11 Product descriptions

1 Authentic listening

a Manufacturing

Basically, we take raw material in the form of steel plate, which is cut into various shapes and then bent and machined to produce individual components. These are then welded together to make what we call the chassis, and that really is basically the framework of the fork-lift truck. To that we then add a mast, which is also made internally here from lengths of channel – that's rolled section – with a hydraulic cylinder. And then the truck is assembled and goes through final testing.

b Fast-food catering

We take a sesame seed bun, place it into a toaster which is temperature-controlled, (and) a slice of meat and, again we put it on to a grill which is temperature-controlled. We dispense accurate measures of both mustard and ketchup, with a slice of pickle and some onions. We put a slice of cheese on it if it's required, then put it into our production bin, which keeps it warm. And then it's served across the counter.

Notes:
Speaker a: the production director of a fork-lift truck manufacturer
'channel' = rolled steel, referred to in the text as 'a rolled section'
Speaker b: the manager of a fast-food restaurant.
The speakers are both English.

2 Shapes

a It's about a foot long – that's about 30 centimetres. It's oval in shape – it's egg-shaped. It weighs perhaps two pounds, about a kilo, and it's made of leather or plastic.
b It's long, maybe a metre long, and quite heavy. It's made of metal, or carbon fibre, or graphite and it's sort of L-shaped.
c It's long, maybe a metre long – that's about three foot. The head is oval, or nearly round, maybe 20 centimetres in diameter.
d It's flat and square, maybe 50 centimetres square and it has 64 squares on it.
e It's triangular, 30 or 40 centimetres across and made of metal or wood or plastic. It has a metal hook at the top of the triangle. It's very light – only a few ounces if it's plastic – maybe a hundred grams.

Notes
Speaker C: says 'three foot'. This is slang for 'three feet'.

UNIT 12 Faults and breakdowns

1 Authentic listening

Speaker 1: An Austrian manager
The system that has recently been installed, which we purchased from your company, works well on the whole. However, we have one problem and that is the address function of the system, which does not allow us to write names and company names in full, which is a very important aspect of our work.

Speaker 2: An American administrator
I'm not very happy with it. It's sending off sparks. It's dangerous because I am using it in the bathroom. Wherever I'm using it, it shouldn't be sending out sparks. And I would like a new model. If you can't replace it with a new model, then I want my money back.

Speaker 3: A Norwegian translator
I think the computer is fine. It's the manual I have problems with. I don't find it is very good. It confuses me. It is not user-friendly, and I don't understand it. I think computer experts simply speak to one another, and not to their customers. The computer was sold as a package to amateurs, and the manual is not for amateurs.

UNIT 13 The services you provide and use

1 Leasing vs. purchasing

To compare leasing with purchasing, we can take the company car fleet as an example. We used to buy all our cars outright, but now we get them on a three-year lease. That way, our expenses are a fixed amount per month, so we can plan, and the leasing company is responsible for all the maintenance and repairs. We used to handle that in-house before. In terms of tax, if you're leasing you can claim the total cost as a business expense.

2 Speakers talking about the help they receive

a I don't have any help at all. We used to have someone who came in to look after the children, but I found it difficult to organise work and home life, and I decided to give up work.
b We employ a cleaner to clean the office. We also have a man who cuts the grass, and looks after the flowers and the car park and does a few odd jobs like that.

- **c** I tend to do everything myself, except anything that involves heights, like the roof or fixing the signs above the window. I really hate heights.
- **d** We have an au pair at the moment. She mainly helps with the children, but she does a little housework as well.
- **e** I don't have any help, which means a lot of things need doing. For example, I must do something about the roof – it leaks every time it rains. I must do something about it.

UNIT 14 Service issues

1 Some complaints

Speaker 1
You promised a 24-hour call-out service. We've been waiting for your engineer for two days now.

Speaker 2
You promised us next-day delivery. That was two days ago and as far as I know it hasn't arrived.

Speaker 3
You said the money would be transferred by the end of the week. It still hasn't arrived.

Speaker 4
You should have let us know immediately. You obviously knew that your stocks were running low and now we've had to stop one of our production lines. How soon can you sort it out?

Speaker 5
Why didn't you tell us earlier that there were no rooms available? We could have made alternative arrangements.

UNIT 15 Service industries

1 Fees and charges

a An investment manager
It's really very simple. I get a percentage of the profits I make. It's a very small percentage, but it's on very large amounts of money. I can't charge expenses, so if it doesn't make a profit, I don't get anything.

b A graphic designer
I sometimes charge an hourly rate. I keep a record of how many hours I've worked, and show the number of hours I've worked there. At other times I'll quote a fee for the entire job. It doesn't matter how many hours I work. And then we agree expenses – that's generally hotels, travel, if I have to go to the clients.

c An architect
Traditionally, our fees have been a percentage of the cost of a building, of the final bill. But clients now, more and more, want a precise cost before they start, and we have to quote on the basis of fixed fees, even including expenses in the quote.

Note
The texts are based on authentic statements.

2 Some company details

- A few words about the company. We now have over 250 contracts in the north-west, and we employ 1,900 people. We have reduced our staff numbers a little since the information which we sent you was written. Our customers are very much the same though. They range from small companies who want us to provide lunch for just a few people up to major employers in the area who require us to provide catering facilities for two to three thousand staff.
- Could you give me some figures? How many meals do you provide, on average, every day?
- About 75,000.
- That's a lot.
- It is, but we have the staff to handle it. They all have to go through a training programme in food hygiene and safety, and all food handling staff have to pass an annual exam which tests their knowledge of nutrition and safety regulations.

UNIT 16 Looking after visitors

1 Authentic listening

a A marketing director
A lot depends on the time of the day, because I think different restaurants are suitable for lunch and dinner. I also think about the nationality of the person I'm entertaining, and what kind of conversation I want with them – whether it's really rather a social occasion. But I think probably the most important thing is that they feel comfortable.

b A partner in a consulting engineering firm
Oh, I would, I would tend to take my clients, for dinner in the evening. We don't tend to take clients to lunch as we used to. In the summer it's very nice to take them for a cricket match at Lord's, or, sometimes we, hire a boat on the River Thames for the evening and entertain in that way. Sometimes we go to the theatre or an opera. So, living near London, we have, a very great deal of choice as to what we do with our clients.

c The managing director of an architectural firm
Our policy on entertaining clients has changed over the years. We have moved from a position where we entertained quite lavishly, to a situation where we try and bring our clients into the office and, over lunch, describe the sort of work that we're actually doing. So they get to know us better. Having said that, we of course do take them out for meals on occasions because we think it's important to actually get a friendship with the people that we're going to work with.

Note
- The speakers are all British.
- Lord's referred to by Speaker b, is a cricket ground (stadium) in London.

2 Planning hospitality

A: Joan, you know we've got a group of people coming over from the Riyadh office next week. Any ideas on where they might like to go? I've been asked to look after them on the Tuesday evening.
B: How long are they going to be here for?
A: Oh, just the Tuesday and the Wednesday. They're arriving early Tuesday morning and leaving at 5 o'clock on Wednesday. Apparently there are going to be five people altogether.
B: I imagine they might like to have a look around the town, do some sightseeing, and possibly some shopping. Then what about a boat trip in the evening?
A: That's what I was thinking. We can arrange a brief sightseeing tour and then take them to the shopping mall. But I think we ought to give them a choice in the evening.
B: That's a good point. They might prefer to have some free time.

UNIT 17 Hotels and restaurants

1 **An evening out**

Exchange 1
- I'm sorry I'm late. The traffic's awful.
- Don't worry, I'm glad you made it. Shall we have a drink before we eat?

Exchange 2
- We'd like to leave our coats.
- And can I leave my briefcase?
- Certainly, madam.

Exchange 3
- What'll you have?
- Let me get them.
- No, tonight you're my guest.

Exchange 4
- Do you want another drink – or are we ready to eat?
- Let's eat.
- OK, let's go through to the restaurant.

Exchange 5
- Good evening. Do you have a reservation?
- Yes, we have a table booked for eight o'clock.
- What name is it, sir?
- Lara.
- Ah yes, this way please.

Exchange 6
- Mario, would you sit there?
- Where would you like me to sit?
- Why don't you sit here, and I'll sit here by the window.

Exchange 7
- What are you going to have?
- I'm not sure, what do you recommend?
- I've heard the seafood is very good here.

Exchange 8
- Excuse me, we're ready to order.
- I'll be with you right away.

Exchange 9
- And what vegetables would you like?
- I'll have broccoli and new potatoes.
- Could I just have a mixed salad, please?

Exchange 10
- That looks very good.
- It smells delicious!
- Well, let's begin or it'll get cold.

Exchange 11
- Cheers!
- Cheers! It's been a good day!

Exchange 12
- More coffee?
- No thank you. Could we have the bill, please?

Exchange 13
- How much should I add on for service?
- Isn't it included?
- I don't think so. How much do you normally leave?

Exchange 14
- How are you getting home?
- Oh, I'll get a taxi.
- Why don't we order one?

Exchange 15
- Could I have my coat, please – it's that grey one.
- Have you got a ticket?
- Er ...
- Like this ...

Exchange 16
- Thanks for a great evening.
- You're very welcome. It was a very useful talk.
- I agree ... Well, good night.

UNIT 18 Corporate entertaining

1 **Authentic listening**

a **A Senegalese technical programme officer**
Being in Dakar, I think the place I would want you to visit would be Goree, which is, er, five miles away from Dakar – an island, where the slaves have been shipped from, to America and other parts of the world. It's a very interesting place and gives you an idea of the conditions in which the people of Africa have been kept before being sent away, I mean, in different places in the world.

b **A Russian civil servant**
Well, first of all, I would suggest that you visit, er, Bolshoi Theatre. I would just take you to opera, or ballet if you prefer. And after that, we could go to (a) nightclub to have some drinks and talk.

c **A Brazilian advertising executive**
Er ... for the night-time, I would like to take you to a restaurant which is very typical. Er, only bar ..., it's a barbecue house. You can eat every kind of meat you can think of, as much as you want, and in the end, you have a kind of a show of carnival. It shows you a bit of what carnival is. It's quite entertaining – you can dance as well, you can join the artists and it's a very good 'vista', you can leave, you can leave Brazil with this feeling inside of you what carnival is, even if you are not there over the carnival time.

d **An Austrian financial controller**
Yes, I understand that you are a lover of music. I would propose that we pay a visit to the Concertgebouw Orchestra House tonight, where they are performing, two wonderful pieces from Austrian composers, Mozart and Hayden. After that, I would suggest that we pay a visit to one of the many Indonesian restaurants here in Amsterdam, where we can enjoy a super reijstafel, which is a speciality of Indonesia.

e **A Dutch customer services manager**
I'm going to take you to the Kirkehof near Lisse. It is, a very beautiful exhibition of all types of spring flowers, especially of tulips, erm, and maybe you've heard of the black tulip – you can see that there as well. And then I would take you to some of the flower markets, because the flowers in the Netherlands are especially very fresh.

Notes

i Some terms
Speaker a: Dakar is the capital of Senegal.
Speaker d: The Austrian financial controller is working in Amsterdam in the Netherlands.
Speaker e: The Kirkehof is a flower exhibition; Lisse is a town in the Netherlands.

ii Non-standard usage

a 'the slaves have been shipped'
(standard usage: the slaves were shipped)
'have been kept'
(standard usage: were kept)
'in different places'
(standard usage: to different places)

b 'Bolshoi Theatre'
(standard usage: the Bolshoi Theatre)
'to opera'
(standard usage: to the opera)

c 'in the end'
(standard usage: at the end)
'show of carnival'
(standard usage: a carnival show)
'feeling ... what carnival is'
(standard usage: feeling ... of what carnival is)

2 Sports vocabulary

a I enjoy all types. I suppose my favourite would be something like the Monte Carlo rally, but I also like Formula One, and the saloon car competitions.

b I usually do about 20 lengths, half breast stroke and half crawl. It's supposed to be good exercise.

c It's a winter sport. You play on grass and it's similar to American football. There are two teams, each with 15 players. It's quite a physical, hard game.

d Snow conditions are usually good in February, and we like to go off piste, so good snow conditions are important.

UNIT 19 Setting up meetings

1 Authentic listening

A French union representative
We have regular monthly meetings with the administration, which take place at an agreed place and time. We, er, at those meetings, we exchange views on a range of subjects which have been put on, an agreed agenda, and, we try, if at all possible, to achieve a common position, and if that is, impossible, we then agree on the setting up of a working group which will look at the subject again.

A New Zealand director of a small real estate company
We have a meeting every May, the Annual General Meeting of the real estate institute. It is a very formal, it has a formal agenda, and it is actively participated in. We also have monthly meetings with our accountant, which usually is, a lunch and a very informal meeting to, analyse what we've been doing and start some planning for the next month.

An Irish export manager
Every month, we have an export managers' meeting, where the export managers, the head of department, and the director, for the department, sit down and discuss pre-set agendas, a very formal meeting ... In contrast, we have an informal, ad hoc team meeting where we discuss the priorities of the week and assess any information that's relevant for the work of the day.

UNIT 20 Meeting procedures

1 Authentic listening

a A Russian civil servant
I don't think so. I am in favour of English remaining to be an international language ... And that's because, the English language is widely used in the world.

b An American administrative assistant
I'm sorry, I can't agree with that statement. English is too widely used throughout the world to be able to drop it as a world language. More and more people – an increasing number of people are being trained in English these days. It would cause tremendous difficulties among many cultures now to replace English with another language.

c A French union representative
I think it should. I totally agree with the proposition that English as a business language is putting a lot of people at a disadvantage. And there is an obvious solution. In the, in the use of an international recognised language, i.e. Esperanto.

d An English production manager
I appreciate what you're saying, but in practice I must disagree, because it would have such a detrimental effect to the whole of the business world because you have so many systems set up using English as the business language.

e A Scottish accountant
I disagree with you completely. A lot of people speak English. It's the most used language.

Notes
Speaker a, non-standard usage: 'remaining to be an international language'
(standard usage: remaining an international language)
Speaker c: i.e. (Latin) = that is/in other words

2 Referring to documents
For example, in the second paragraph, second line, what is the word at the end of the line?

a If you look near the bottom of the first column, it says, 'until the very end of the meeting'. What is the next word?

b In the second column, first line, a name is mentioned. What is 'it'?

c In the last paragraph, there is reference to a Robert Townsend. It says he is a guru. What is the word before 'guru'?

d In the middle of the second column, it states that Stalin 'then invited comments'. In the next line, what is the first word?

e Finally, what's the second name which is mentioned below that?

UNIT 21 Meeting follow-up

1 Authentic listening

An American marine pollution engineer
Well, I think the most important thing is to have a well-understood and clear agenda, and to end it on time. If you put everyone under a time constraint, then they'll – they'll reach their conclusions quicker and probably eliminate a lot of talking that's unnecessary.

A French union representative
I think that what makes a successful meeting is a combination of factors. The most important, in my opinion, would be preparation. It is essential that those taking part know exactly the

subject and have, worked on the background. The second is probably the approach taken by the chairman – his ability to direct the discussion. And, finally if you're looking for a successful outcome, probably the willingness of most participants to compromise.

A Dutch customer services manager
Oh, I think the most important thing is to have a good agenda and stick to it and also to limit the meeting to a certain number of people, because if you get a very large meeting it will be very difficult to get all the points through. Of course, at the end of the meeting, you – you will want to have the feeling that you've covered all the points, that you have good action points – so that makes it useful to get good minutes. Of course, you need someone who really knows how to chair the meeting and who also makes sure that no one takes too much time and discusses certain subjects at too great a length.

Note
Dutch customer services manager: non-standard usage: 'to get all the points through'
(standard usage: to get through all the points)

UNIT 22 Arranging a visit

1 **Authentic listening**

a **A German lawyer**
If you come from Hamburg, you have to go through the whole town of Rostock. First, cross a big roundabout. Then go straightaway through the whole town until you reach a bridge at the other end of the town. After the bridge, you go left into a road which is called The Strand, and er, and half of the length of the road, you find our office directly at the road, and, it's a big building made from red stone, so you can't miss it.

b **An American engineer**
You'll be coming from Anchorage to Valdez. It's a journey of about 315 miles with one turn, one right-hand turn. You get on Route 1, which is the Glen Highway. Travel for approximately 200 miles; take the only right turn available to you; and travel for another 115 miles and you'll be in Valdez. Take a left turn at the Shell station and you'll come right to my building.

c **A Sri Lankan working in Rome**
Yes, from, the Termini station, if you take Line B, or Linea B, you'll ... The third station is Circo Massimo. So when you come, come out of the, underground station you'll find, find our building on the right-hand side.

d **A Swedish manager**
Well, when you arrive to Arlanda, you have a couple of different possibilities, but I think the best thing would be to take a bus that goes from Arlanda every 20 minutes into central Stockholm, and it stops by the train station. And that's also where the underground station is. So you go from the bus station into the underground station and you take a tube that goes to Mariavik. It's the blue line on the underground and it will take you about 10 to 15 minutes. So in all, you should count on about one hour from the airport to my office.

Notes

i Place names
- Hamburg/Rostock are cities in Germany.
- Anchorage/Valdez are towns in Alaska, USA.
- Termini/Circo Massimo are train stations in Rome.
- Arlanda is Stockholm's main airport. Mariavik is an underground station.

ii Non-standard usage
- **Speaker a:** 'go straightaway through'
(standard usage = go straight through)
'go left into a road' (standard usage = turn left into a road)
'half of the length of the road'
(standard usage = halfway down the road)
'you find'
(standard usage = you will find)
- **Speaker d:** 'you arrive to Arlanda'
(standard usage = you arrive at/in Arlanda)
'count on about one hour'
(standard usage = allow about one hour)

UNIT 23 Abroad on business

1 **Attitudes to foreign travel**

Speaker 1
The easy thing is that you can concentrate 100% on the task. I suppose the difficulty is that it is tiring: you have to adjust to a lot of different people in an environment that isn't your own, and possibly use a language that you're not particularly proficient in.

Speaker 2
I think the hardest thing to cope with when you're travelling is not knowing where things are. Even when you move into the company offices, everything's in a different place. And you don't have the back-up and support that you have when you're in your own organisation. I actually enjoy all the travelling, but you have to be fairly well organised and make sure you've got the tickets and you know exactly where you need to be and when. The thing I don't like is if you run out of time and you're running late for flights. Then I find I get very flustered and everything is much more tiring. And you do get more tired when you're travelling abroad – it is tiring travelling.

Speaker 3
Well, the things I like about travelling overseas are meeting new people, seeing new towns, new places, and tasting strange food. Things that can get a little wearing are spending weeks by yourself in hotels, and certainly as far as Far East travel is concerned, the long flights, which can be exhausting.

2 **Everyday travel situations**

1 – What number is it?
– 217; it's a company called Albas Mining.

2 – How far is it to Fawley?
– About 80 kilometres, but the eastbound carriageway is closed after junction 8, so there might be delays.

3 We're still trying to trace your luggage. It seems it was loaded on the wrong aircraft.

4 You can park in the basement – the entrance is just behind the hotel.

5 – Can I have an early call, in the morning?
– Certainly, what time?

6 The rental includes unlimited mileage and comprehensive insurance cover.

7 You can get a bus to the centre from just outside the building. Then take the subway to Mariavik – the entrance is next to where the buses stop.

8 – There's one at 8.22 that gets there at 12.47.
– What time is the one after that?

UNIT 24 Returning from a business trip

1 Discussing a business trip

Speaker 1

It was a very short trip. It was only two and a half days, and I went to Almaty and Astana in Kazakhstan. And the purpose of the trip was to talk to our distributors about progress last year, this year, and to plan promotion for the forthcoming year. I went with some new colleagues because I wanted to introduce them to our distributors. So, it was part business, part social, in fact.

Speaker 2

Well, my last business trip was a very short trip to Paris – I just went for two days. And the idea of it was – was to have a promotional lunch with, potential users of our latest product. And it actually went very well indeed and – and a certain amount of business was done over lunch, which was a nice informal way of doing it.

Speaker 3

My last business trip abroad was to Istanbul, to present a design to a major bank over there. We presented the design and we also presented the fee, and we hoped that as a result of that, we would win the job. However, what we heard today was that we're still one of two for the next stage of the competition.

2 Acronyms

For example.

– They receive a subsidy from the EU.
– Do you mean that it's funded by the European Union?
– Yes, that's what I was told.

a – They're a member of OPEC.
– I'm sorry, but what's OPEC?
– The Organisation of Petroleum Exporting Countries.

b – The WHO is interested in the scheme.
– Do you mean the World Health Organization?
– Yes.

c – It's a decision by the IMF, the International Monetary Fund.

d – NAFTA was formed in 1993.
– What does NAFTA stand for?
– I believe it's the North American Free Trade Agreement.

e – I'm sorry, but I don't remember what ASEAN stands for.
– It's the Association of South East Asian Nations.

UNIT 25 Personal finances

1 Comparing prices

– How do prices in Iceland compare with those in the UK? I've heard that Iceland is an expensive country.
– Yes, it always has been, but at the moment the pound is quite strong against the krona, so things like eating out in restaurants and staying in hotels are cheaper than they used to be. But eating out is still quite expensive, and drinks cost about twice as much as they do in the UK – a bottle of wine in a restaurant is expensive. But I don't mind paying the prices – the fish is fantastic as you would expect, and the lamb is wonderful. Food in the shops is not cheap, probably on average about one and a half times more expensive than in the UK.
– Do you manage to get out much, or do you spend all of your time working when you're there?
– I try to get out and see as much of the country as possible, yes. I like to go fishing when I have the chance – Iceland is a great place for fishing. Last time I was there I did actually manage to find some time to drive up to the fishing port at Akranes – I'm not sure how you pronounce it – from Reykjavik. I went out on a boat and caught quite a lot of fish, for once – mainly cod and haddock. To get to Akranes you have to drive past some fantastic mountain scenery. You really should go to Iceland if you have the chance. I don't know anywhere else like it.

2 Fractions and multiples

For example. Our last claim was for $2000, but this one will be three times that.

a We expected about 8,000, but it was half of that.
b We estimated about 2,000, but it's twice as much as that.
c Her salary is about 2,000, and his is about double that.
d We thought about 8,000, but it's not more than a quarter of that.
e We thought about 4,000, and it's similar to that.
f We estimated about 6,000, but it's much, much more than that.

UNIT 26 Company finances

1 Authentic listening

a A Scottish computer sales executive

Business is still quite difficult, and the recession has bitten quite hard. But I think most people are now beginning to see some improvement in business and our numbers are beginning to look a bit better than they were last year – the recession is beginning to lift. Forecasts for next year are looking quite good and there seem to be a lot of longer-term projects coming to fruition, which should help the numbers no end next year.

b An English manager of a fast-food chain

Financially, we're doing very well. Over the previous year, we have increased our sales by £139,000, which is about 6.39%. To increase that even further, especially in this economic climate, we've got to increase our market share, and to increase our market share we must make more people aware of what we are doing – a different type of promotion, for example, a new idea, or taking a successful promotion and re-running it.

c An English partner of a consulting engineering firm

Last year, we probably had our best year from a profits point of view in the firm's history. The market then was booming and, we didn't have to look very far for work. But in the last 12 months, the UK water industry has stopped its spend on capital works, and consequently things are going to be quite difficult this year. We are in fact looking further overseas for work in order to make up the shortfall.

Notes

Speaker a: numbers (colloquial use) = sales figures
Speaker c: spend = spending
capital works = major investments
shortfall = the amount not achieved

2 Financial statements

Speaker 1

The group has produced a good performance in the last year despite very difficult trading conditions, especially in the food and drink sectors. Trading profit increased by 12.3%. Total trading profit amounted to £1,009 million.

Speaker 2

I am very pleased to report on another successful year. The accounts at 30th June show that the total sales made by the group were $3,397 million – some 7% higher than last year. These sales, producing the same margins as last year, created a trading profit of $362 million, an increase of 6%.

Speaker 3

As we all know it has been a disappointing year for the company, mainly as a result of lower-than-expected sales. Our trading profit of £32.4 million is however down by only 3% compared with last year. We are confident of a significant upturn in sales next year.

UNIT 27 Payment issues

1 Mathematical terms

- **a** The cost will be between twelve and thirteen hundred.
- **b** Three-quarters of the population are employed.
- **c** The office is about a hundred square metres.
- **d** The dividend will be three hundred and fifty-two divided by two point seven.
- **e** It's ninety-nine point nine nine per cent pure.
- **f** The cost will be thirty-seven dollars fifty times thirty-six.
- **g** Its capacity is about five and a half cubic metres.
- **h** The profit is two point oh six million minus one point seven three million.
- **i** The units are fifteen ninety-nine each.
- **j** This is a query about your invoice number one three six stroke D.

UNIT 28 Preparing for a presentation

1 Presentation checklist

Speaker 1

It is very important to check everything very carefully. You need to check all the equipment that you're going to use. You should, if you can, go and have a look at the room to see what size it is – you need to know exactly how many people are involved, what their level of interest is. But I think the most important thing is to check the technical equipment, to make sure that you know how it works, because it's very difficult when you're using a bit of equipment for the first time not to be thrown by it. And to simply think through everything that you're doing and make sure that you've got a logical sequence. I think that's probably about it.

Speaker 2

The most important thing about presentations is to familiarise yourself with the room that you're actually going to present in, whether it's your own office or whether it's the client's office. So, if it's the client's office, we always try and see the room before the presentation, so that we can check out the seating arrangements. We also think it's important to have a trial run, so that we can test the time of our presentation related to our client's schedule.

Note

Speaker 1: to be thrown by = to be confused by.

UNIT 29 Presenting facts and figures

1 Referring to a graph

- **a** The heading in the top left-hand corner reads 'domestic sales'.
- **b** The figures from zero to 200, each represent a thousand dollars.
- **c** The bottom line axis shows six months, starting April and ending September.
- **d** The straight line at 100,000 shows the average value of sales from April to September.
- **e** To complete the graph. Sales at 160,000 in July remain steady, with no change for August. Sales for the following month, for September, then drop sharply to one hundred thousand.

UNIT 30 Delivering a presentation

1 Stages in a presentation

- **a** With regard to the figures, this table shows projected sales for the coming year. If you look at the column on the left, you will see that they are divided into ... Can everyone see that OK? ... Yes? ... Good ... They are divided into columns ...
- **b** ... in the staffing levels. That brings me to my next point. But first, are there any questions so far? No? So, moving on, we're ...
- **c** ... to be here. First, I'll give you a brief overview of the position, and then I'll say a few words about the takeover. As you know, the company has ...
- **d** Three years ago the company appointed a new chairman. Two years later, profits reached a record figure of 345 million. The company began a period of global expansion ...
- **e** ... there'll be time for more questions after coffee. Now, I'll hand over to Michael Soras, because he'd like to say something about the product range. Michael, over to you ...
- **f** ... That's a good question – the problem of job security is something I cover in detail in the second part of my talk. So if you don't mind, I'll say more about that later ...

Track List

CD 1

Track	Unit	Page	Activity
1	1	5	Some Useful Phrases
2	1	6	Act. 1, Act. 2
3	2	7	Some Useful Phrases
4	2	8	Act. 1
5	3	10	Some Useful Phrases
6	3	11	Act. 1, Act. 2
7	4	12	Some Useful Phrases
8	4	13	Act. 1, Act. 2
9	5	15	Some Useful Phrases
10	5	16	Act. 1, Act. 2
11	6	18	Some Useful Phrases
12	6	19	Act. 1, Act. 2
13	7	21	Some Useful Phrases
14	7	22	Act. 1, Act. 2
15	8	24	Some Useful Phrases
16	8	25	Act. 1
17	9	27	Some Useful Phrases
18	9	28	Act. 1, Act. 2
19	10	30	Some Useful Phrases
20	10	31	Act. 1, Act. 2
21	11	33	Some Useful Phrases
22	11	34	Act. 1, Act.2
23	12	36	Some Useful Phrases
24	12	37	Act. 1
25	13	38	Some Useful Phrases
26	13	39	Act. 1, Act. 2
27	14	41	Some Useful Phrases
28	14	42	Act. 1
29	15	44	Some Useful Phrases
30	15	45	Act. 1, Act. 22

CD 2

Track	Unit	Page	Activity
1	16	47	Some Useful Phrases
2	16	48	Act. 1, Act. 2
3	17	50	Some Useful Phrases
4	17	51	Act. 1
5	18	54	Some Useful Phrases
6	18	55	Act. 1, Act. 2
7	19	57	Some Useful Phrases
8	19	58	Act. 1
9	20	60	Some Useful Phrases
10	20	61	Act. 1
11	21	63	Some Useful Phrases
12	21	64	Act. 1
13	22	66	Some Useful Phrases
14	22	67	Act. 1
15	23	69	Some Useful Phrases
16	23	70	Act. 1, Act. 2
17	24	72	Some Useful Phrases
18	24	73	Act. 1, Act. 2
19	25	74	Some Useful Phrases
20	25	75	Act. 1, Act. 2
21	26	77	Some Useful Phrases
22	26	78	Act. 1, Act. 2
23	27	80	Some Useful Phrases
24	27	81	Act.1
25	28	83	Some Useful Phrases
26	28	84	Act. 1
27	29	86	Some Useful Phrases
28	29	87	Act. 1
29	30	88	Some Useful Phrases
30	30	89	Act. 1